Living and Working in
Spain

*The complete guide to a successful
short or long-term stay*

ROBERT A. C. RICHARDS
2nd edition

howtobooks

To Myrtle Allen of Fowey, Cornwall, with thanks again for giving me the first lesson in writing.

Published by How To Books Ltd,
3 Newtec Place, Magdalen Road,
Oxford OX4 1RE, United Kingdom.
Tel: (01865) 793806. Fax: (01865) 248780.
email: info@howtobooks.co.uk
http://www.howtobooks.co.uk

Second edition 1998
Reprinted 1999
Revised and updated reprint 2001
Reprinted 2002

British Library Cataloguing in Publication Data.
A catalogue record for this book is available from
the British Library.

Cover design by Baseline Arts Ltd, Oxford

Produced for How To Books by Deer Park Productions
Typeset by Kestrel Data, Exeter
Printed and bound by Cromwell Press Ltd, Trowbridge, Wiltshire

NOTE: The material contained in this book is set out in good faith for general guidance and no liability can be accepted for loss or expense incurred as a result of relying in particular circumstances on statements made in the book. Laws and regulations are complex and liable to change, and readers should check the current position with the relevant authorities before making personal arrangements.

Living and Working in Spain

Contents

List of Illustrations

Preface

Why is Spain different? That is best known to a very-full-time press correspondent and writer, who has been living in Spain since 1963. The answer is fully given in this book, so read on.

The following chapters detail the realities of 'living and working in Spain', and describe those many differences which make life more pleasant . . . as well as the disadvantages.

Many customs in Spain are unlike those in other countries. For example, the fixed habit in general is a very light breakfast, then a large, *late* lunch and dinner. Why? Amando de Miguel explains in his book *Los Españoles* that it stems from past centuries. 'The peasants ate a hearty breakfast, and went to bed early. The nouveaux riches wished to be as different as possible, hence went to bed very late after dinner, and took their siesta after a delayed lunch.'

Many facets of lifestyle are described in this book, and there is an extensive chapter on holidaying in Spain with traditional offers, and new ones. Full answers are given to questions such as: What is the greatest danger in Spain? How do the Spanish drive? How can you avoid traffic fines? How can you breakfast your way around Spain in luxury surroundings? How do you stay healthy/wealthy/wise? And even how do you make carrot cake?

With full travel details and scores of helpful tips, this book provides vital information for anyone moving to Spain, whether to work for large companies or in a self-employed capacity. There is also plenty of sound advice – and some warning notes – for the large numbers of people hoping and planning to move from the UK to live in Spain after retirement.

This book pulls no punches, but shows the real *España*. Reading it will spare you many expensive and unpleasant experiences. It will definitely help you to fit comfortably into the Spanish way of life, besides enjoying brief holidays in Spain more fully.

Robert A. C. Richards

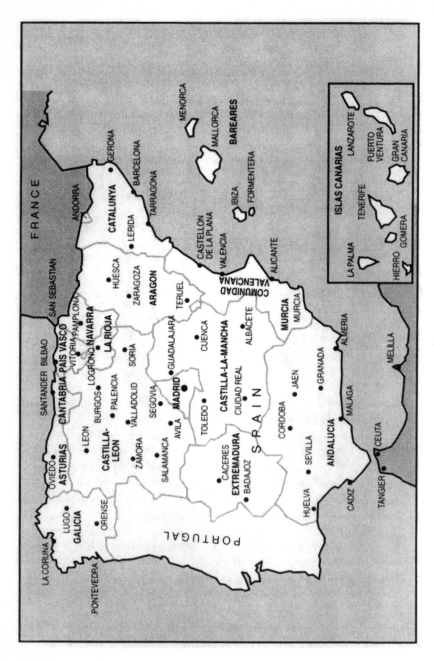

Fig. 1.   Spain: regions, provinces and main cities.

1

Arriving in Spain

You will be made to feel welcome when you arrive in Spain. The customs officer at the border will smile at your children – they are the rulers of the roost throughout Spain. The taxi driver at the airport is often a mine of information. And the climate smiles, too. Gone are the days of 'rain spreading from the west' as day upon day of cloudless skies dawn.

The Spanish way of life offers everything from classical guitar played in ancient castles to a multitude of modern hyper and supermarkets. In Madrid and many other cities, ancient monuments cluster next to modern high-rise buildings, although nowadays care is taken to protect these memories of a vast, ancient and well-documented history. Streams of different peoples have left their permanent mark from the Iberos of uncertain origin to the Romans who provided monuments in every part of the Peninsula. The Spanish saga includes the Visigoths, a surprisingly long Arab occupation, and the *reconquista* when the northern kingdoms finally completed the domination of Spain in 1492.

DECIDING WHETHER SPAIN IS FOR YOU?

When planning any project, it is good to sit down in a quiet corner to determine exactly what is involved. Here are a few really basic questions worth considering.

Living in Spain

- Do I want a better climate – and can I stick the weather? The heat and high humidity can be very trying.

- Can I adapt to the Spanish timetable with its late lunch and evening meal and shopping hours which last until 22.00?

- Am I fond of company or do I have a Greta Garbo complex? – both can be accommodated.

- Can I adapt to the extrovert life, so very different from the Northern European reserve?

- Can I learn a foreign language when I have so many other commitments? (You will never be able to enjoy living and working in Spain to the full unless you do!)

Working in Spain

- Would I be prepared to work in the evening?

- Could I adapt to a variable working timetable?

- Would I be prepared to work non-stop from 08.00 or 09.00 until 15.00 (*horario intensivo*) during the very hot summer months?

- Could I work the standard multinational timetable, when the rest of the country is operating on a different wavelength?

The quirks of the country
Spain is different in many unexpected ways from other countries. The next chapter is devoted to a detailed description of just *how* different. You should consider it carefully when making your decision.

KNOWING THE COUNTRY

Hundreds of thousands of people from the EU and elsewhere have made Spain their retirement home, after starting with a holiday residence. The weather normally helps this decision, and Spain is a welcoming country. You are made to feel welcome – as described by many foreign language newspapers and magazines which greatly help would-be 'settlers' (see pages 24 and 25). Mainland Spain has much to offer, again described in this chapter, including full travel details. You could even copy the Romans, who settled all of the Iberian Peninsula and, besides numerous remains, left their city names – and generally they chose the best places to live.

The Roman influence
Long before the Arabs came to conquer Spain in the eighth century, the Romans had discovered many of the fine points of the country. Their villa sites are located in pleasant areas besides

rivers and coasts. Remains can be seen in every part of Spain from the leafy greenness of Asturias to Mérida with its impressive theatre, amphitheatre and aqueduct.

Some modern Spanish place names remain unchanged like Segovia, others are similar like Tarragona, originally Tarraco, and Málaga, formerly Malaca. Others are completely different but that is not to say that the Roman names have fallen out of use. If someone tells you he is '*complutenses*', it is not contagious; he means that he is a native of Alcalá de Henares. They are also used in written Spanish in lower case as above. This is the correct *castellano* which is spoken in the region of that name, particularly in the cities of Valladolid, Palencia and the ancient university of Salamanca. Here is a table to help you identify these places.

Modern city name	*Roman city name*	*Spanish adjective*
Astorga	Asturica Augusta	asturicenses
Cádiz	Gades	gaditanos
Calahorra	Calagurris	calagurritanos
Calatayud	Bilbilis	bilbilitanos
Ecija (Seville)	Astigi	astigitanos
Elche (Alicante)	Ilici	ilicenses
Gerona	Gerunda	gerundenses
Gibraltar	Calpe	calpetanos
Huelva	Onuba	onubenses
Huesca	Osca	oscenses
Jativa	Saetabis	setabitanos
Lérida	Ilerda	ilerdenses
Lugo	Lucus Augusti	lucenses
Málaga	Malaca	malacitanos
Mérida	Emerita Augusta	emeritenses
Palencia	Palantia	palentinos
Salamanca	Salmantica	salmanticenses
Segorbe (Castellón)	Segobriga	segorbinos
Seville	Hispalis	hispalenses
Tarragona	Tarraco	tarraconcenses

Examining regional differences

Whether you are in Spain for a long or short stay it should be remembered that it has a massive mainland – 491,205 square kilometres – with a wildly different character in each of its seventeen autonomies. The exploration of inland Spain is simple and well worth the time and effort. The wide variation of regional characteristics is a true part of the 'Spain is different' claim of so many travel posters. Compare this to the statement made by a Greek gentleman – 'We have visited every part of the British Isles, and it's all the same. The architecture is the same in Scotland as in Cornwall, with Marks and Spencers everywhere, and a standardised form of housing.' Although much the same could be said of the modern parts of Spanish cities, there is usually an extensive ancient portion as well which is full of individuality.

The *Costas* are so well documented in travel literature of every sort that there seems little point in repeating them. Instead the unique qualities of the fifty provinces in Spanish territory will be noted here.

The provincial capital cities all have the same layout. There will be the ancient centre with its medieval buildings, often including a 'PN' (*Parador Nacional* or State-run hotel), surrounded by a pleasant modern shopping centre. Then, on the outskirts, there will be the uniform blocks of flats and even a few detached houses. Until recently the Spanish have always considered the community life of modern high-rise flats as the most desirable form of residence but these days the latest craze is for separate housing. These range from matchbox units in terraces to luxury detached dwellings.

If you prefer to visit areas less well known to foreigners try the north-west where the historic cities of Ávila, Salamanca, Zamora, Orense and Pontevedra are to be highly recommended for their highly individual character. Their Paradores Nacionals are often converted castles, monasteries, or other ancient buildings.

While being expensive, they can make a delightful stay for several days; or just . . . breakfast, as travellers are welcomed for all.

Here is a quick guide to a few select provinces.

Extremadura
The cities of Cáceres and Badajoz are well worth seeing as are other 'ancient jewels' such as Mérida (founded by the Romans in 25 BC as Augusta Emerita and also known as the 'Rome of Spain'), Zafra, Guadalupe, Trujillo, Alcántara, Plasencia.

Cataluña
As Cataluña is one of the most industrialised parts of Spain, it is not surprising that you have to travel a certain distance to escape from its development, but the country areas are very pleasant.

The ancient homes of gentleman farmers have frequently been converted into luxury restaurants serving the traditional cuisine in high cool rooms. The PNs (State hotels) are to luxury standards, thus indicating a good tourist area. PN Vich overlooks lakes, and is located in quiet, wooded countryside . . . postcode 08500. Tel: (93) 888 72 11, fax: (93) 888 73 11. The PN of Cardona is an impressive castle with fine views . . . postcode 08261, Tel: (93) 869 12 75, fax: (93) 869 16 36.

Barcelona

Barcelona caters for every taste. There are ample beaches nearby, an extensive marina in the port, boat trips and motor racing at Montjuich, the huge Olympic village. Its nightlife is famed for its catholic appeal, from classical concerts and the best opera singers, jazz festivals and rock and roll concerts to the guitars in the cafés and the litre-sized glasses of beer to be bought in the old plaza near the port. The Catalans may be famous for their hardworking characteristics but they also know how to enjoy themselves.

The city of Barcelona offers a great deal to the visitor or resident. The port area attracts many to see the replica of Columbus' ship, enjoy the palm-lined gardens and sample the *tapas* in the bars. You can climb to the top of Columbus' statue, erected on the site near the Plaça del Rei where he is reputed to have given his first report after his return home to the *Reyes Católicos* (The Catholic Monarchs). Guidebooks and booklets are as numerous as editions of foreign newspapers here and they will tell you all about it. Museums abound. The Poble Espanyol is another very interesting place. Here you will find each region of Spain represented by a house built in the traditional, regional style of that province. From these houses you can buy goods traditionally associated with the provinces.

Nevertheless, the very high temperatures and humidity experienced in the hottest months of July and August can make staying in Barcelona very unpleasant. You can make plenty of trips out though to escape the conditions.

The coastline

The coast is the obvious choice in the hottest months. It is the choice of many Catalans, too, so expect traffic jams at peak periods. Blanes marks the start of the *Costa Brava* (Wild Coast), so-called because the coastline is so rough. To the north there are many *calas* (rocky coves) with clear waters and bright sands.

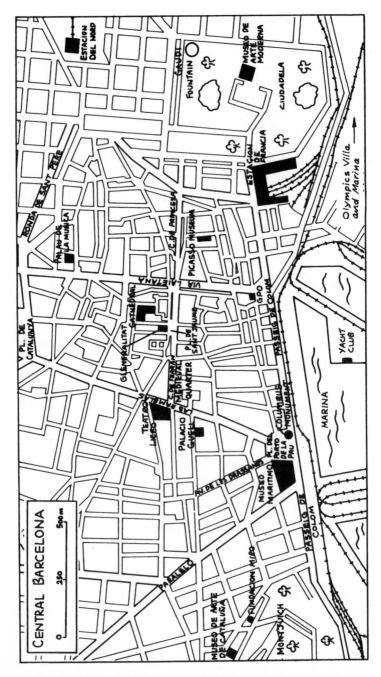

Fig. 2.   Barcelona street plan.

Blanes is 106 kms from Barcelona and offers fine beaches and the Marimurtra. This is not a tame dragon but a botanical garden with over three thousand species of flora. It overlooks the rocky coast and is an ideal place to enjoy the sea breeze. Its name means 'sea and myrtle'.

Blanes is the place where the coastal scenery changes. To the south, there is flat country and rather unattractive beaches; to the north lie the many coastal resorts so well served by the charter airport of Gerona. It may be very difficult to find enough space just to sit down in Tossa de Mar but the tourists continue to flock in their thousands. Lloret de Mar is pleasant as is the ancient port and holiday resort of Pálamos. For sheer five star luxury, the PN of S'Agaro is to be recommended. The coastal road may not have been designed for busy travellers but the constantly changing views are delightful. Rosas is a large resort with a good beach and a fishing village.

Cadaqués was the hometown of the surrealist painter Salvador Dalí. It is isolated by twisty roads but worth visiting. The old theatre where Dalí held his first exhibition as a teenager has been converted into a museum in his honour. It is as eccentric as the painter's own creations. The opening hours are just as eccentric, from 17.00 until 21.00 on alternate days. There is a complicated schedule of guided tours so if you plan to visit this museum you would be well advised to telephone in advance.

South of Barcelona the beaches are long and flat and there are a variety of resorts. Castelldefels has pleasant housing developments and little else. Sitges, however is an older resort with its own character, good beaches (topless), and a reputation for being the place to go. Villanueva y Geltrú is a small family resort with a large fishing port where many foreign concerns are investing. Tarragona is a bustling provincial capital with good beaches, many hotels, and an impressive Roman theatre.

For those who enjoy motorway travel, Peñíscola and Sagunto are ancient cities, very pleasant and full of history. Vinaroz is an unpretentious family seaside resort. Its weekly street market is remarkable for the low prices of local, freshly harvested fruit and vegetables.

Andorra

Although this is a principality and not part of Spain it must be mentioned. Over 50,000 people live here in tax-free glory. Some residents claim to get to Barcelona in two and a half hours using the

Cadi tunnel. Besides being a mecca for tax-free shopping, Andorra
has utopian mountain valleys, excellent skiing stations, and many
other attractions – especially its tax-free status. There is a PN at Seo
de Urgel which boasts an impressive interior patio hung with plants
and you can also enjoy a swim in the indoor swimming pool. This
hotel incorporates the cloisters of a monastery. The postcode is
25700. Tel: (973) 35 20 00, fax: (973) 35 23 09.

Andalucía
Seville hosted a World Exhibition in 1992. In anticipation, the
Hotel Alfonso the Twelfth, first built for another giant exhibition
held in 1928, was totally refurbished at a cost of 2,000 million
pesetas to full five star, super-luxury standards by Ciga Hotels
España. The city of Seville can keep you busy sight-seeing for
many days but Andalucía with its white villages, *bodegas* (wine
cellars) and folk-lore has its attractions too.

Among the numerous Roman remains to be seen are the ruins
of Itálica, only 7 kms to the north of Seville, and the necropolis at
Carmona.

Écija, 89 kms to the east of Seville is known as *la sartén de
Andalucía* (the frying-pan of Andalucía). It lives up to its name
with temperatures of 50°C in the shade in July and August. The
heat is something to consider if you do plan a trip to this area
and is something most guidebooks neglect. If you like the heat,
and want to see eggs literally fried on the pavement, then visit
Ecija in high summer when the *astigitanos* will be glad to give
you a demonstration. Otherwise the best months are April and
October.

In Jerez de la Frontera there are many *bodegas* which welcome
visitors, and the Equestrian School which, though perhaps not to
the standard of Vienna, gives demonstrations of horsemanship
and the stables can be visited afterwards. Arcos de la Frontera is a
picturesque town. Cádiz is an ancient port and city whose narrow
streets give a welcome to all and can be seen by horsedrawn
carriage.

Ronda just must be seen by anyone visiting Andalucía. A
spectacular bridge links the two rocky headlands on which the
town is built and there is the oldest bull ring in Spain. It is an
ancient town with streets of excellent restaurants such as the Don
Pedro. The Hotel Victoria is furnished in a severely English style
and has a palm-shaded garden commanding a spectacular view of
the valley below and the river Guadelevin. On the floor of the

gorge between the two parts of the town lie the ruins of *la Casa del Rey Moro* (the house of the Moorish King) from which Christian prisoners were made to carry water to the town up 365 stairs, a height of 100 metres – hence the saying and curse: *'en Ronda mueras acarreando'*, ('May you die in Ronda carrying water barrels'). Ronda now has a new, attractive PN.

There are other cities in Andalucía which really should be visited, the most usual being Granada, Córdoba and Málaga. Doñana is a nature reserve of over 80,000 hectares, where you can see wild boars, lynx, deer, many rare birds, huge flocks of migrating flamingos, sand-dune 'creep', long unspoilt beaches, pine forests and all sorts of other wildlife. What you see largely depends on the time of year so it is better to check in advance if you wish to visit.

The headquarters building is open every day except Monday from 08.00 until 19.00. You can enjoy a guided tour by Land-rover but you must book in advance. The address is El Acebuche, Coto Doñana (Huelva), Tel: (955) 43 04 32.

Remembering Columbus
At the Monasterio de la Rábida near Palos de la Frontera, Christopher Columbus awaited the backing of the *Reyes Católicos* for his westerly voyage to the Americas. Most of the original monastery was destroyed in an earthquake in the seventeenth century but the existing one is pleasant. A priest will take you on a guided tour and tell you all about that famous day, 12 October 1492, when a cannon shot from Columbus' flagship, *La Pinta*, echoed across an empty ocean. It signalled the first landfall and greatest development scheme ever.

CONSIDERING THE ADVANTAGES OF LIVING IN SPAIN

The Spanish timetable has much to recommend it. Whenever you wish for refreshment, whatever the time, it is almost always possible to find somewhere, particularly in the cities where there are 24-hour services. Even in the smaller towns, many catering establishments are open from 06.00 until midnight – unless it is the local closing day. Spanish barmen work at a speed second to none; they really try to please and earn every bit of their free time . . . and tips (which are expected).

Café society

This is very much a part of living in Spain. The entire family will go to the nearest bar or café, from the youngest to the oldest, to enjoy a drink and the evening breeze. Sometimes the family go for a full Sunday meal after which a siesta is essential. The Spanish love to talk and this greatly extends their mealtimes. However, the average Spaniard believes that time should be his servant rather than his master and the Mediterranean attitude of not worrying too much about the future prevails.

Taxation in Spain

Rates of taxation are still lower in Spain than in many countries. Tax on an average middle class income may still be lower than in the UK. Social security, however, is quite high. The tax and social security contributions on the average income of an employee are shown in Figure 3 on page 21. It works out much better, however, for the self-employed.

If you are self-employed you must declare all the income earned in whatever country if you stay in Spain for more than 183 days per year. You start out by paying 20 per cent tax on it but at the end of the tax year the *Hacienda* (tax office) will refund any excess. In this way, after many moons, real taxation works out at 10 per cent, and you have a compulsory saving scheme.

Since the EU seems determined to standardise taxation this will doubtless change for the worse. Remember, too, that all income is taxed, even pensions.

Taxes on cars and boats are usually lower in Spain than in other countries. There are no hidden taxes on televisions or radios either. Some homes boast a dozen radios and more, with a television set for every member of the family.

Service charges

Bills for water, rates, electricity and so on are often lower than in northern Europe. However, if you decide to buy a flat it is better to choose one with separate heating rather than the very expensive collective heating systems used by some communities of proprietors. Community of proprietors (*comunidad de propietarios*) is the term used for all the owners of apartments or flats in one building and they are subject to much legislation about which there are many books.

0010/0051

EMPRESA					N.° INSCRIP. SEG. SOCIAL	N.I.F. o C.I.F.

DOMICILIO		POBLACION

TRABAJADOR			N.° AFILIACION SEG. SOCIAL	N.I.F.	GPC 1271 07

FECHA ANTIGUEDAD	N.° MATRIC.	EPIGRAFE	CATEGORIA	PTO. TRABAJO	PERIODO DE LIQUIDACION	TOTAL DIAS
13-01-9X		113	AUX. ADVO.	1.47	AGOSTO 9X	30

CUANTIA	PRECIO	1 (*) 2	CONCEPTO	DEVENGOS	DEDUCCIONES
		1	SALARIO BASE	72187	
		1	AUMENTO LINEAL	37957	
		1	GRAT. VOLUNT. ABS.	5091	
			APORT.TRABAJ. SS. 4,70 %		6345
			APORT.DESEMPL.FP. 1,70 %		2295
			I.R.P.F. (115235) 8 %		9219

(sidebar) (*) 1 PERCEPCIONES SUJETAS A COTIZAC. AL REG. GEN. DE LA SEG. SOC. 2 PERCEPCIONES EXCLUIDAS DE COTIZAC. AL REG. DE LA SEG. SOC

DETERMINACION DE LAS BASES DE COTIZACION AL REG. GEN. DE LA SEG. SOCIAL

BASE TOTAL DE COTIZACION		DESGLOSE BASE TOTAL	IMPORTE	TOTAL DEVENGADO	TOTAL DEDUCIR
REMUNERACION TOTAL	115235	CONTINGENCIAS COMUNES	135000	115235	17859
PRORRATA PAGAS EXTRAS	18849	DESEMPLEO y F.P.	135000	97376	
TOTAL	134084	HORAS EXTRAS		IMPORTE TOTAL A PERCIBIR	

FECHA	FIRMA Y SELLO DE LA EMPRESA	RECIBI. (Firma del Trabajador)
31-08-9X		

Fig. 3.   A typical Spanish monthly payslip showing salary for the month, with social security and taxation deductions.

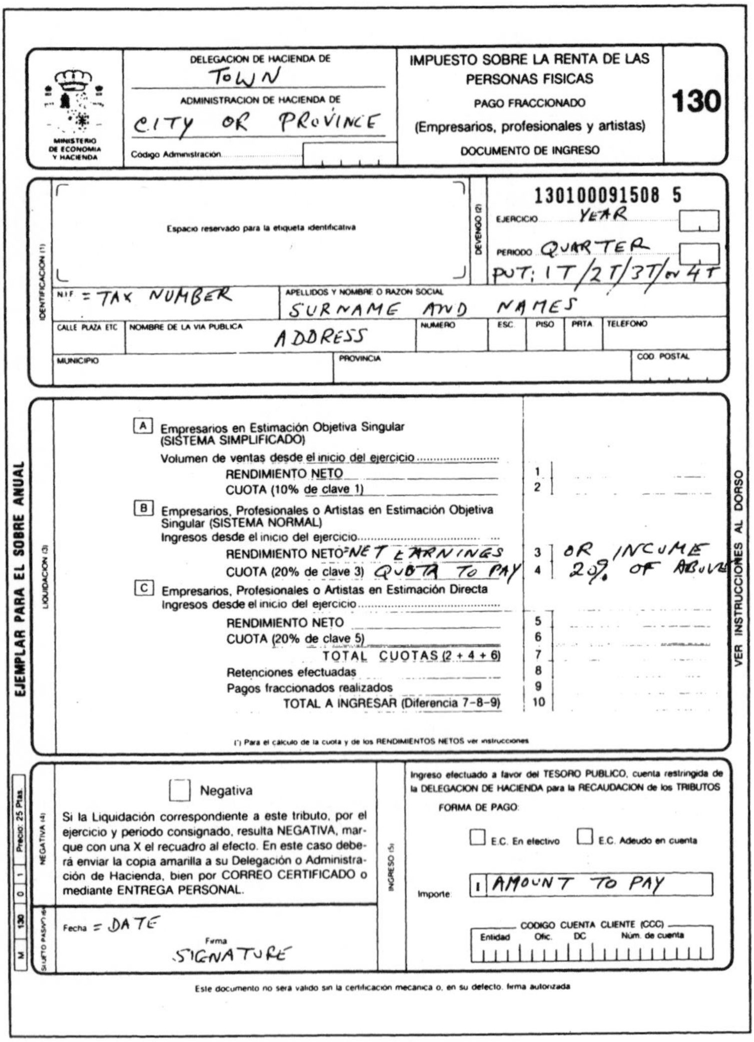

MINISTERIO DE ECONOMIA Y HACIENDA

DELEGACION DE HACIENDA DE TOWN

ADMINISTRACION DE HACIENDA DE CITY OR PROVINCE

Codigo Administración

IMPUESTO SOBRE LA RENTA DE LAS PERSONAS FISICAS

PAGO FRACCIONADO

(Empresarios, profesionales y artistas)

DOCUMENTO DE INGRESO

130

IDENTIFICACION (1)

Espacio reservado para la etiqueta identificativa

DEVENGO (2)

130100091508 5

EJERCICIO YEAR

PERIODO QUARTER

PUT: 1T/2T/3T/or 4T

N.I.F. = TAX NUMBER

APELLIDOS Y NOMBRE O RAZON SOCIAL: SURNAME AND NAMES

CALLE PLAZA ETC	NOMBRE DE LA VIA PUBLICA	NUMERO	ESC	PISO	PRTA	TELEFONO
	ADDRESS					

MUNICIPIO	PROVINCIA	COD POSTAL

EJEMPLAR PARA EL SOBRE ANUAL

LIQUIDACION (3)

A Empresarios en Estimación Objetiva Singular (SISTEMA SIMPLIFICADO)

Volumen de ventas desde el inicio del ejercicio

RENDIMIENTO NETO — 1

CUOTA (10% de clave 1) — 2

B Empresarios, Profesionales o Artistas en Estimación Objetiva Singular (SISTEMA NORMAL)

Ingresos desde el inicio del ejercicio

RENDIMIENTO NETO = NET EARNINGS — 3 — OR INCOME

CUOTA (20% de clave 3) QUOTA TO PAY — 4 — 20% OF ABOVE

C Empresarios, Profesionales o Artistas en Estimación Directa

Ingresos desde el inicio del ejercicio

RENDIMIENTO NETO — 5

CUOTA (20% de clave 5) — 6

TOTAL CUOTAS (2 + 4 + 6) — 7

Retenciones efectuadas — 8

Pagos fraccionados realizados — 9

TOTAL A INGRESAR (Diferencia 7–8–9) — 10

(*) Para el cálculo de la cuota y de los RENDIMIENTOS NETOS ver instrucciones

VER INSTRUCCIONES AL DORSO

NEGATIVA (4)

Negativa

Si la Liquidación correspondiente a este tributo, por el ejercicio y periodo consignado, resulta NEGATIVA, marque con una X el recuadro al efecto. En este caso deberá enviar la copia amarilla a su Delegación o Administración de Hacienda, bien por CORREO CERTIFICADO o mediante ENTREGA PERSONAL.

SUJETO PASIVO (6)

Fecha = DATE

Firma SIGNATURE

INGRESO (5)

Ingreso efectuado a favor del TESORO PUBLICO, cuenta restringida de la DELEGACION DE HACIENDA para la RECAUDACION de los TRIBUTOS

FORMA DE PAGO:

E.C. En efectivo

E.C. Adeudo en cuenta

Importe I AMOUNT TO PAY

CODIGO CUENTA CLIENTE (CCC)

Entidad Ofic. DC Núm. de cuenta

M 130 0 1 Precio: 25 Ptas.

Este documento no será válido sin la certificación mecánica o, en su defecto, firma autorizada

Fig. 4. Tax Form 130 for the self-employed. The form costs 25 ptas. Rendimiento neto = net earnings. The self-employed will normally complete just section B, paying a quota of 20% tax.

Rubbish is collected every day of the week except Sunday and you have to pay a small fee for the service. If you need a photocopy you will find a machine in most newsagents as well as in the special shops which offer reductions in price.

NOTING SOME DISADVANTAGES

General grumbles range from the deficiencies of the telephone service to the worst public services in Europe. Talking to local people is the best way to discover specific drawbacks. Chapter 3 will give you a good idea of some of the major differences of Spain and some of the trials you will face if you work in Spain.

Crime

The authorities take crime very seriously. Anything from someone trying to sell you yesterday's newspaper to your shopping trolley moving away all by itself. Thefts of car radios and cars are commonplace as are burglaries. Constant vigilance and precautionary action go a long way towards counteracting this.

Lying is an accepted part of life in Spain, so do not believe everything you are told. Whether the result of the official religion promulgating 'the pious lie' for so many centuries or part of the third world mentality that still exists in much of Spain, the practice is common and expertly carried out. It is extremely trying to come up against it in officialdom.

FINDING OUT MORE ABOUT SPAIN

One way to prepare for your move is to obtain the local newspaper or magazine published in English (many are also produced in German, French, Scandinavian languages, etc.). They are normally packed with news, information and advertisements, and put you 'in the picture' very rapidly.

The *Sur in English* is the 'grandfather of them all', with a long history and print run of about 30,000 every week. It is published from their HQ in Málaga in the centre of the Costa del Sol. Their list of clubs covers most activities and pastimes, from politics to cross country running, cricket, etc. The numerous meeting places of fifteen religions are fully detailed, including Muslim, Jewish, Jehovah's Witnesses, Den Norske Kirke and Bahai. This publication normally appears in English, but they occasionally have special issues in German or other languages.

A recent report by SOPDE and the Andalusian Federation of Property Developers and Foreign Residents (which appeared in *Sur*) stated that in the Province of Málaga alone, the investment by foreigners is worth some 3,000,000 million pesetas or half the holiday homes available. Those number about 100,000, and they produce an annual income of around 800,000 million pesetas (mpts). Foreigners thus have a very strong invested interest in the area, and rightfully a say and vote in local politics. Hence the large number of foreign language publications, such as *Sur* and others in the following list.

Foreign language publications produced in Spain

Sur in English, Avenida Doctor Marañón 48, 29009 Malaga. Fax: 952 61 12 56. Tel: 952 64 96 67, 952 64 96 92. E-mail: sureng@surinenglish.com. Internet: http://www.surinenglish.com.

The Broadsheet, calle Emilio Rubin 5 Bis, Chalet 4, 28033 Madrid. Tel: 91 721 94 76. Fax: 91 759 68 58. Gives very good coverage of the Madrid scene, amusements and way of life.

Focus on Spain, World Link Communication SL, calle Rio Tago 74, 28600 Boadilla del Monte (Madrid) idem. Tel: 91 632 01 39. Fax: 91 632 20 91.

Editur, Ediciones Turisticas SA, Gran Via Carlos III 66, 7 08028 Barcelona. Tel: 93 330 70 52. Fax: 93 330 74 96. Weekly/travel.

Info Magazin Verlag, calle Huertas 26, 38700 Santa Cruz de La Palma, Canary Isles. Tel: 922 41 52 00. Fax: 922 41 55 16.

Costa Blanca News, calle Doctor Pérez Llorca 3, Edificio Astoria, 03500 Benidorm. Tel: 96 585 52 86/87. Fax: 96 585 83 61.

Weekly Post, PO Box 95, 03500 Benidorm. Tel: 585 52 86/7. Fax: 96 585 83 61.

The Reporter, Avenida de Suel 23, Pueblo López, 29640 Fuengirola (Malaga). Tel: 95 246 86 45, 95 246 50 86. Fax: 95 246 71 04. E-mail: thereporteraalsur.es.

Journal la Gaviota, Apartado (=PO Box) 2013, 03500 Benidorm (Alicante). Tel: 96 680 38 86. Fax: 96 680 21 02. French bi-monthly. Office in El Centro, Avda.de Europa.

Guia d'Andorra, PO Box 135, Principat d'Andorra. Tel: 9738 26 770. Quarterly in English, French, Catalan and castellano.

Spain Gourmetour, Paseo Castellana 14, 28046 Madrid. Tel: 91 431 12 40. Fax: 91 431 61 28.

Costa del Sol News, Apartado 95, 03500 Benidorm (Alicante). Tel: 96 585 52 86/7. Fax: 96 585 83 61. Every Thursday.

La Gazeta Magazine, Apartado 574, 03590 Altea (Alicante). Tel: 96 579 46 77.

Costa Golf, calle Loma de los Riscos 1, Apartado 358, 29620 Torremolinos (Malaga). Tel: 952 38 15 42.

Island Gazette Magazine, calle iriarte 43, Puerto de la Santa Cruz, Tenerife, Canary Isles. English.

The Entertainer, Apartado 414, 04630 Garrucha (Almeria). Tel: 950 478 850. Fax: 950 478 789. Two weekly editions – Andalusian Edition and Costa Blanca Edition, plus *The Entertainer Online* at www.tcom.co.uk/online/

SOME HIGHLY RECOMMENDED TRIPS

These trips are based on the city of Madrid. You can either stay in Madrid and make a series of excursions on a daily basis or make slightly longer trips staying overnight. Where possible, accommodation has been recommended. If you visit any of these places you will be sure to discover the real *España*. Descriptions of places are given in case you are short of time and may only see a few of them.

Madrid
This city has been the capital of Spain since 1606 and has acquired many palaces, museums, parks and avenues over the years. The Retiro park is ideal for a lunchtime snack in the summer months,

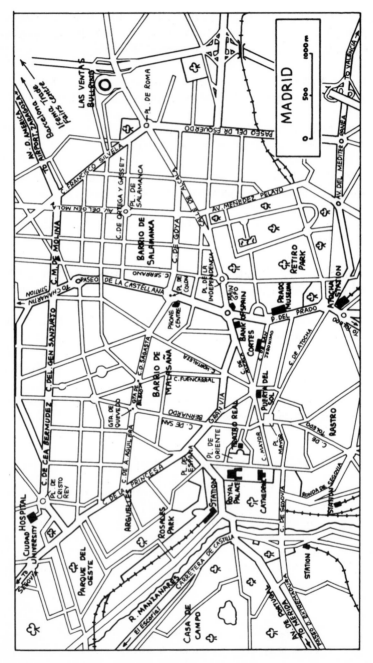

Fig. 5. Madrid street plan.

and is well policed. The Prado museum houses the finest collection of Spanish paintings in the world, and nearby the Thysen Museum also has an impressive collection. The Royal Palace is impressive, used solely for occasions of State. The King lives in a modest palace on the outskirts – the Zarzuela.

Toledo

Toledo captures the essence of inland Spain with a wealth of ancient buildings, including two synagogues which are well worth visiting. El Greco's house can be visited and many other monuments. The famous Alcázar began as a fortress in Roman times and was nearly destroyed in the Civil War when it withstood a seventy-two day siege. It has now been restored.

El Escorial

The huge royal palace is usually described as a monastery and was built by Felipe II between 1563 and 1584. It gives the impression of massive and ageless strength, the main buildings covering a rectangle of 207 by 161 metres. There is a museum beneath it which demonstrates the construction methods of the time: models of wooden cranes used to hoist huge blocks of stone into place and the original tools. The palace has many important works of art and a famous library.

There are several mini-palaces worth seeing too. There is one near the railway station and another on the road to Avila. It is pleasant to wander about this little town with its open-air cafes and restaurants of all grades, and La Herreria, the park. The Hotel Miranda Suiza makes a pleasant place to stay.

El Escorial is about 1,000 metres above sea level and can make a pleasant change in the summer from Madrid which is only some 600 metres above sea level. The surrounding mountains are covered with pines and are good hiking and walking country. So is the Sierra de Malagón.

Close to El Escorial is the Valle de los Caídos. This is the impressive burial site of General Franco. He lies under a huge granite slab in an interment on the scale of a Pharaoh. Some of his followers treat the tomb as a shrine.

Incidentally, in winter, El Escorial is well known for icy winds which rush down the mountain sides causing snowfalls which have been known to make roofs collapse. In winter, you should wrap up warmly, as sub-zero temperatures are not uncommon. Many local inhabitants keep snow chains in their cars. The same can apply to Madrid and many a winter visitor from northern Europe has been caught shivering in a thin raincoat while the natives wear thick overcoats, gloves and scarves.

Ávila

The ancient city of Ávila is worth visiting to see its encircling walls and ancient buildings. The walls were built in the eleventh century when King Alfonso VI conquered the city in 1085 and settled the land with people from the north. The walls are high with a perimeter of some 2,500 metres and include eighty-eight towers and nine well-preserved gateways. Inside there are many ancient buildings including a pleasant PN where a good breakfast may be enjoyed in a large dining room. For other meals there is a good *à la carte* menu.

Ávila is the highest provincial capital in Spanish territory, being 1,126 metres above mean sea level. Thus it often heads the list of cities with the lowest temperatures during the winter. This also applies to the summer when some visit to avoid the stifling heat of Madrid and enjoy sleeping under a blanket. The street market is held on Fridays, the cattle market on Tuesdays. Both are worth seeing.

Aranjuez

The river Tagus helps to cool the environment here. It flows through the grounds of the royal palaces to which the monarchy used to retire in summer. Aranjuez is worth visiting to admire the Royal taste, the extensive gardens and the town. There are plenty of shops and stalls which offer two famous local products (in season) – strawberries and asparagus. A special train runs from Madrid during which journey attractive hostesses in period dress will offer you free strawberries. On arrival the town band will greet you while the steam locomotive refuels (beware of getting covered in soot!)

Alcalá de Henares

Roman remains abound in this city which was known then as Complutum. The city has recently been declared a national monument and is receiving a three million pound facelift, backed by EU grants and aid. The city claims to have the longest under cover walkway in Spain (in its main street), and boasts many ancient colleges and buildings. Its university was founded by Cardinal Cisneros in the sixteenth century and can be visited.

Directly behind it is the luxury restaurant, Hostería, where Cervantes, the writer of Don Quixote, is said to have dined as a student. Cervantes was, in fact, born here and the register of his baptism has been carefully preserved and frequently reproduced.

You will find another sixteenth century relic here, the *Biblia Polyglota Complutense*. Cardinal Cisneros commissioned this Bible and it is in four languages. The first bride of Henry the Eighth of England, Catalina de Aragón, was born in this city as was Fernando I. The university thrived here until one fine day in 1836 it was moved to Madrid. After this the city (now some 170,000 in population) declined. It was hit badly during the Civil War but is now enjoying a renaissance and is well worth a trip. To get to Alcalá de Henares you should take the motorway towards Barcelona and you will find it just past Barajas airport, 30 kms from Madrid. There is now a special train from Madrid to this city with guided tours available. The local tourist offices can give details.

The Hotel Bedel beside the old University building and Plaza de Cervantes makes a good place to stay.

Guadalajara

The provincial capital of Guadalajara lies 30 kms further on towards Barcelona. Here the Palacio del Duque del Infantado is to be found. It used to belong to the powerful Mendoza family during the fifteenth, sixteenth and seventeenth centuries. References to the Mendozas occur frequently in history, among them many VIPs and land developers of the Americas. Also among them was that Cardinal Mendoza who had so many 'natural' sons and daughters that a special reception and fiesta would be given for them every two years. As a result of these Queen Isabel I of Castilla came to know his *bellos hijos* (beautiful children) who apparently ran into scores.

One of those *bellos hijos* was called Martin Gitano because his mother was a *gitana* (gypsy). He was the ancestor of that Miguel de Cervantes who, besides writing Don Quixote, had time to travel widely, distinguish himself in the naval battle of Lepanto when he lost an arm and spent many years as a Corsair prisoner in North Africa waiting for his ransom to be paid. This man was a writer, adventurer, traveller, poet, and playwright. He even died on the same day as Shakespeare – 23rd April 1616.

Chinchón

The similar word *chichón* means a bruise in Spanish but there is nothing bruised about the appearance of this little village, famous for its central plaza where a weekly street market allows you to buy every type of fruit and vegetables as well as clothing and a variety of farmers' goods. Old houses with arched balconies ring the square. The balconies are used as grandstands when bullfights are held right in the centre of Chinchón. Many houses have been converted into restaurants and bars as this is a popular day trip for the *madrileños*. It is 50 kms from Alcalá de Henares on country roads and about 40 kms from central Madrid.

There is a passable PN with a large garden, fountains, pools, and numerous very productive fruit trees. This makes a pleasant, quiet day out and you can take home a bottle of anis liqueur or wine from the *Bodega Cooperativa San Roque* which produces wine with the Vina Galindo trademark.

Puerto de Navacerrada

This is Madrid's ski resort with one Nordic and twelve Alpine ski runs. Ski-able altitude is from 1,700 to 2,222 metres above sea level. All kinds of catering facilities are available from a thirty-room hotel to a seventy-five-room hostel. All the necessary equipment may be hired *in situ*. 'Night skiing' now operates here.

It is a popular drive from Madrid and at times most of Madrid appears to be trying to park there, cars blocking the sole access from the south, the N-601. However, there is another access approached by taking the main highway to Burgos, the N-1, then turning left just past Lozoyuela, and taking the C-604 to Rascafría. At Rascafría there is a good *parador*-type hotel where you could stay. The road continues to the Valcotos ski station where there is ample space, or, if you prefer, you may continue to the crowded slopes of Navacerrada. Here the road peaks at 1,860 metres and then leads on to Segovia and the attractive summer palace of La Granja.

La Granja

Versailles will immediately come to mind when you enter the extensive gardens of this summer palace. That was the intention of its builder, Felipe V, the first Bourbon king of Spain (1683–1746) and the great grandson of Louis XIV of France. Terrace slopes rise upwards with elaborate fountains and watercourses. If you are very lucky you may arrive on one of the few days of the year when these are turned on. They are a kingly sight. The gardens are still used for State occasions.

The palace has some excellent sculptures and other works of art. At an altitude of 1,192 metres it provides a breath of coolness in the Spanish summer and makes the surrounding pine forest popular for picnics (*comidas en el campo*) with many *madrileños* and visitors who come from all over everywhere. When you tire of the palace, you may follow the road to Segovia with its fairytale palace.

Segovia

The name Segubia first appears in records of the second century BC, thus being established before the Roman legions marched in and built the aqueduct. The aqueduct continued to be used for its original purpose until the beginning of this century bearing witness to the quality of Roman engineering. Although modern traffic is having an adverse effect on its structure the aqueduct still stands and keeps the eyes of tourist cameras firmly focused on this impressive creation, half a mile long.

Nearby there are many restaurants specialising in the regional favourite of roast piglet. The roast lamb is very good too.

The Alcázar, Segovia's fairytale palace, began life in the twelfth century and is, perhaps, Spain's most photographed castle. If you climb one of the corkscrew staircases to the upper watchtowers you will be rewarded with a view of *La Mujer Muerta* (The Dead Woman). This is a mountain range which resembled the body of a reclining woman with its two peaks, La Pinareja, 2,193m, and Oso, 2,192m.

Riofrío

On the way back to Madrid by car you will pass this Sierra and the royal palace of Riofrío which is housed in an attractive deer park. The deer come up to the car for bread and other offerings. The palace was built by the wife of Felipe II, Doña Isabel de Farnesio, and was also the home of Alfonso XII. Besides the royal relics it contains an interesting display of regional fauna and flora.

Back to Madrid

The N-603 highway soon joins the *Carretera de La Coruña* which is usually crammed with traffic on Sunday evenings and Monday mornings, and evenings after holidays. A fine view may be obtained from the mountain pass called *El Alto de los Leones*, at 1,156 metres high, but when the temperatures are sub-zero, its sharp gradients can be dangerous and it is better to take the toll tunnel. Guadarrama is the next village with a wide range of eating places, even take-away roast chicken. Then you can go straight back on the motorway – traffic permitting – to Madrid.

2

Sampling the Highlights
of Spanish History

The 'United States of Spain'? This has been the objective of legislators ever since the death of General Franco in 1975 and for this reason: Spanish territory has been divided into seventeen regions, each having its own regional government, complete with a *Presidente* and variable number of ministers known as *consejeros* or regional variations of the title. The regional government has authority over public works, education, sanitary services and the like. The most powerful regional governments such as those of the Basque Region, Galicia and Cataluña even have their own police forces and tax collectors. They are generally more powerful than the other regions, reflecting the ancient kingdoms on which the regional divisions were made. Although there is a federal system it does not yet match that of the United States. However, the idea exists and may well forge a link between modern Spain and its long and turbulent history.

A GLIMPSE OF PRE-ROMAN SPAIN

The Celts and the Iberos
The Iberos were the first to settle in the ancient Spain of classical times. They may have originated in the *Iberia Caucasica* (Africa). The principal tribes of the Iberos and their settlements were:

- the Cántabros in the area around Santander and Cantabria

- the Carpetanos in the area around Toledo

- the Ausetanos, Indigetes, Ilergetes, Ilergavones, and Layetanos north of the River Ebro

- the Contestanos and Edetanos in Valencia

- the Mastienos and Deitanos in Murcia

● the Tartesios, Bastetanos and Oretanos in Andalucia

● the Lusitanos in Portugal.

You will still come across some of these names, like *Cántabros*. The Via Leyetana is also a principal thoroughfare in Barcelona. Greek and Roman writers mention the Tartesios and their king Argantonio who reigned from 630 BC until 550 BC.

The Celts crossed the Pyrenees and invaded Spain in about 1200 BC, receiving further reinforcements in the sixth century BC. The Celts seem to have bypassed the Basque country. The Basque people seem to date from well before this period and the language defies all attempts to trace its origins. The principal tribes of the Celts and their associated regions were:

● the Artabros and the Calaeci in Galicia

● the Berones in La Rioja

● the Turmódigos in Burgos.

The two races of the Celts and the Iberos became well mixed throughout the remainder of the Iberian Peninsula. The result was the Celt-Iberic population and culture, an example of which is the *Dama de Elche*, the head of an ancient goddess found in south-east Spain in 1897. The principal Celt-Iberic tribes and areas were:

● the Arevvacos in the upper part of the River Duero

● the Belos in Medinaceli (famous for a unique Roman arch)

● the Lusones in Daroca and Calatayud (Zaragoza)

● the Pelendones in Soria

● the Titos in Segorbe (Castellón).

The Celt-Iberos built fortified cities which were, in fact, city states. At times they united to fight common enemies. There is some evidence that all these tribes were governed by a senate of elders or princes and kings. The largest was the Tartesios.

Although the Celt-Iberos settled much of the Iberian Peninsula, others such as the Phoenicians colonised ports and other areas. King Argantonio of the Tartesios encouraged other peoples to establish colonies in Denia (Artemisión), Mainake (near Málaga), Corduba, Abdera and other locations.

All these states co-existed relatively peacefully.

However, when King Argantonio died, the Tartesios attacked the Phoenicians at Gadir (Cádiz) and began a round of wars which continued until the Roman occupation.

Carthage rules

The Phoenicians were quick to summon aid from their allies, the Carthaginians who established their first base in Ebusus (Ibiza) about 550 BC. The war went so well for the Carthaginians that they ended up ruling Cádiz and all the land around the southern and eastern coasts to the River Ebro. The Carthaginians eventually made a treaty with Rome that this would be the frontier. Later when Hannibal wished to make war on Rome he attacked the fortress city of Sagunto, some 30 kms to the north of Valencia.

THE ROMANS

Sagunto withstood a long siege, but eventually the inhabitants made the same decision as the Jews of Masada and chose to die rather than surrender. The siege ended in 218 BC but marked the beginning of the Second Punic War. Sagunto had signed a friendship treaty with the Romans and two hundred years of warfare began. The Roman war machine moved into top gear and utilised every means to conquer the Iberian Peninsula. The final battle of the war was waged against the last remaining Celt-Iberos, the Asturs and Cántabros. Caesar Augustus headed seven legions to defeat the remnants, successfully establishing the *pax romana* for nearly five hundred years. Four Roman emperors were born in Spain: Trajan, Adrian, Maximus and Theodosius. The provinces augmented in number from the original three, Bética, Tarraconse, and Lusitania to include Balearica, Gallaecia, Cartagunense and Tingutana.

At this point, between 19 BC and 15 BC, Zaragoza which had appeared in 550 BC as an Iberian walled city, was founded as a Roman city by Caesar Augustus and named Caesaraugusta after him. The veterans returned here from the Cantabrian war, the Fourth Legion (Macedon), the Fifth Legion (Alauda), the Sixth Legion (Victrix) and the Tenth Legion (Gémina).

The city of Caesaraugusta became an important Roman metropolis with four gates – Valencia, Toledo, Angel and Cineja. They were linked by the main streets of Cardo Maximus and Degvamnus Maximus. In 460 AD, the city was still flourishing under Roman rule when Emperor Majorianus visited it.

Just twelve years later it fell to an army of Goths commanded by Count Gauterico, and Roman supremacy was swept away by the armies of the Visigoths, Suevos and Franks.

CHRISTIANS AND MOSLEMS

By that time, Christianity was well established in Spain in spite of an inauspicious beginning. Christianity had been taken to Spain by road and ship and had met with severe persecution throughout Roman Spain (*Hispania*). The Pro-Consul, General Sergio Suplicius Galva, published his imperial edict banning the faith and Gayo and Cremencia, the first martyrs, met their deaths in Zaragoza in 66 AD.

By the fourth century AD Zaragoza had become a base for evangelising, helped originally, perhaps, by the apostle Paul who mentioned that he intended to visit Spain in Romans 15:24, 28. Whether he did or not, you may see his statue at Tarragona celebrating his visit!

In 711 AD the Arabs invaded Spain under General Tariq ibn Ziyad who gave his name to Gibraltar (*Gibel–Tariq*, rock of Tariq). The general and his hosts used the Roman roads to sweep past the Visigoth resistance (which was greatly divided) and rapidly dominated the Iberian Peninsula. In the spring of 714 AD, Zaragoza was taken by Mussa, and its name changed to Sarakosta. Spain came under Arab domination and was declared an emirate. Arab domination in the eighth century extended to France, Poitiers being the farthest point north when the Arabs battled unsuccessfully with Charles Martel in 732 AD.

The far north of the Pyrenees was freed from Moorish occupation very quickly, by 737 AD, as was Asturias and Cantabria. This explains why the peoples of these regions have the most European appearance today. Exactly the opposite applies in the south of Spain where the Arab occupation lasted until the end of the fifteenth century. Visiting a bar in some parts of rural Andalucia may be similar to visiting a north African bar as far as the physiognomy of the occupants and occasionally, the character.

Zaragoza was returned to Christendom on 18 December 1118 AD when Alfonso I, *el Batallador*, conquered the city. He used his northern army of Bearnese, Borgonese, Aquitanos, Navarros and Aragonese to defeat the forces of Ali ben Yussuf, part of the process of overthrowing the Moors which lasted until 1492 AD when Granada was conquered.

The Arab occupation of Spain brought great benefits to Spain by introducing Arab art and craft and establishing important universities like the one in Córdoba, the southern capital.

The Reconquista (Re-conquest)
This word occurs millions of times in books devoted to Spanish history. It is used to describe the period of fighting between 722 AD after the Battle of Covadonga (721 AD) and 1492 when the Catholic Monarchs (*Los Reyes Católicos*) took the last Moorish stronghold, Granada.

During the 781 years that the Arabs controlled the Iberian Peninsula, battles were waged back and forth, with alternate advances by Arab then Christian forces. Gradually the Christian kingdoms of the north emerged as Aragón, Asturias, Cantabria, Cataluña, León, Galicia, Navarra, Castilla (this is much of central Spain and takes its name from the great number of castles (*castillos*) built at that time). It is hard to calculate which areas belonged to which force at any period of time since some areas like León changed hands several times.

In the meantime in the south, rival factions divided the Arab world with the result that Spain was split into Arab kingdoms which grew smaller and smaller. This gave the Christians the opportunity to advance. If you are interested in Spanish history there are a great many books available on the subject and a surprisingly large number of original documents have survived. If you only have a passing interest, the outline of its history detailed here will help you appreciate the background of the many ancient and historic buildings that you will see.

On 2 January 1492, King Fernando II of Aragón and Queen Isabel I of Castilla and León won the final victory over the Moorish forces at Granada. Spain had, at last, acquired national unity, which had been the monarchs' intention since their marriage in 1469 at Valladolid. They sent a letter on 2 January to communicate the news to the *Consejo de Zaragoza*. It took thirteen days to arrive and the victory was celebrated with special processions on 15, 16 and 17 January 1492. Pope Alexander VI gave the monarchs the title of *Los Reyes Católicos* as a reward for their achievement.

King Fernando II of Aragón proceeded to extend his dominions in many directions and his full title is Fernando V of Aragón, Castilla, Sicilia and Napoles. He lived from 1452 until 1516 and was one of those rare individuals who seemed to know how to govern the unruly Spanish.

1492 was as fatal for the Jews in Spain and Portugal as it was for the Arabs. Many thousands of them were expelled and they fled to places as far apart as Wales, North Africa and Jerusalem. They speak a form of Spanish which dates from the fifteenth century and can be rather hard to understand. It is called Sephardim and you may still hear it in special programmes on Hebrew radio stations. Some Sephardic families still possess the original key to the homestead they were forced to leave in 1492. Today, friendship programmes exist in Spain and the *Sefardies* are frequent visitors, holding conferences in their former capitals such as Córdoba and Toledo.

CHRISTOPHER COLUMBUS AND LOS REYES CATÓLICOS

1492, as has been mentioned elsewhere, is also the year the greatest land development voyage of all times concluded: Christopher Columbus made the first recorded landfall in the Americas on 12 October 1492. Altogether Columbus made four voyages across the Atlantic during the course of which he discovered San Salvador, Haiti, Cuba, other Caribbean islands and the coasts from the Orinoco to Caracas.

However, recent evidence gives the honour of the first landfall in the Americas to the Vikings. They established villages in Newfoundland centuries before Columbus – but that is another story.

The complete records of his voyages have been preserved and make interesting reading. The first was written by Fray Bartolomé de las Casas. He records that Columbus would never tell his crew exactly how far they had travelled each day because he did not want the actual distance to frighten them. When Columbus landed on the island called *Guanahani* (the first day of the discovery of the New World), Fray Bartolomé noted the beauty of the nude natives greeting them and remarked that none seemed older than about thirty.

The record of the second voyage was written by Columbus and given to don Antonio de Torres to give to *los Reyes Católicos*. He also made the records of the third and fourth voyages. He liked to be called *El Almirante* (the Admiral), a title which his descendants still use.

Although *Los Reyes Católicos* backed Columbus at first, Court intrigues later disgraced him. He died in near poverty, in Valladolid on 20 May 1506 and left two wills which can be seen today. They are dated 22 February 1498 and 25 August 1505. The second will bequeaths various sums of money to many people in Genoa: Antonio Vazo, Luis Centurión Escoto, '*Jerónimo del Puerto, padre de Benito del Puerto, Chanceller en Génova*' and *Paulo de Negro, genovés*.

If you mix with Spaniards at all you will soon hear a reference to *huevo de Colón* (Columbus' egg). The story is told in all parts of Spain and goes as follows:

'One day Columbus was with some of his enemies who tried to make little of his great exploits. So Columbus asked them to balance an egg on end on the table. All tried without success. Then Columbus tapped one end of the egg and balanced it easily (presumably it was hard-boiled like the ones you see in Spanish bars today). They all replied that it was too easy and simple – but Columbus replied with an ironic smile, "but it did not occur to you first." '

MONARCHY AND REPUBLIC

The Habsburgs
Carlos I was the first Habsburg king and he came to the throne in 1516. He is remarkable for having founded the '*Archivo de Escrituras Reales*' in 1509 to record deeds of castles, titles and all royal business matters from mines to rents. This collection, now known as the *Archivo de Simancas*, is kept in Valladolid and numbers 33 million documents, or so it is claimed. The last Habsburg king died in 1701 and Felipe V came to the throne.

The Bourbons
Carlos III was the most notable of the Bourbon kings. He reigned from 1716 until 1768. He is considered to have been one of the best Spanish kings. He established a Golden Age to the benefit

of the population. As you travel around Spain you will see many of this king's architectural creations.

Fernando VII restored Bourbon rule in 1814 after the Napoleonic occupation. As a result he was known as *El Deseado* (the Desired). However, he tore up the 1812 Constitution and became a tyrant. After that he was known as *El Rey Felón* (the King of Treachery). This restoration like some subsequent restorations of Bourbon rule was not a happy event.

The nineteenth century in Spain was characterised by the struggle between liberals and conservatives with varying degrees of success. Isabel II reigned from 1843 until 1868 when a republic was established by revolution.

In 1875 Bourbon rule was restored when General Martínez-Campos proclaimed Alfonso XII the next Bourbon monarch in January 1875. His reign was prosperous and peaceful for many Spaniards but it only lasted for ten years. He died of tuberculosis (as did his first wife) at the age of 28 in 1885. His second wife produced an heir posthumously, Alfonso XIII. There was a costly regency period during which Spain lost the last of its American possessions, Cuba, Puerto Rico and the Philippines, in 1898.

MODERN POLITICAL LIFE

Alfonso XIII ruled from 1906 until 1931 when he was forced to exile himself to Rome. The republic which succeeded him until 1936 (when the Civil War began) was violent in every way.

When the Civil War ended in 1939, liquidisations followed for the losers and years of starvation. The victors lived well under Generalísimo Franco who lasted until 1975. In this year Bourbon rule was restored once more with King Juan Carlos and Queen doña Sofía, excellent monarchs, and very popular in Spain today.

The change to Bourbon rule after the dictatorship of Franco came more calmly than many observers believed possible and King Juan Carlos I immediately showed that he is a great believer in democracy. He receives all the party chiefs whether Communist or right wing.

In fact, the first elections brought a centre party to power which was headed by Adolfo Suàrez. He cleverly manoeuvred the country through the difficult times of great change. However, he decided to resign after a military take-over bid on 23 February

La Línea dinástica española

1. **Vermudo I** de Cantabria, Rey de Asturias en 788 AD
2. **Ramiro I**, Rey de Asturias, padre de
3. **Ordoño I**, Rey de Asturias, padre de
4. **Alfonso III**, Rey de Asturias, padre de
5. **Ordoño II**, Rey de León padre de
6. **Ramiro II**, Rey de León, padre de
7. **Ordoño III**, Rey de León, padre de
8. **Vermudo II**, Rey de León, padre de
9. **Alfonso V**, Rey de León, padre de
10. **Sancha** Reina de León, casada con Fernando I de Castilla, padres de
11. **Alfonso VI**, Rey de Castilla y de León, padre de
12. **Urraca I**, Reina de Castilla y de León, casada con Raimundo de Borgoña, padres de
13. **Alfonso VII**, Emperador y Rey de Castilla y de León, padre de
14. **Fernando II**, Rey de León, padre de
15. **Alfonso XI**, Rey de León, padre de
16. **Fernando III**, Rey de Castilla y de León, padre de
17. **Alfonso X**, Rey de Castilla y de León, padre de
18. **Sancho IV**, Rey de Castilla y de León, padre de
19. **Fernando IV**, Rey de Castilla y de León, padre de
20. **Alfonso XI**, Rey de Castilla y de León, padre de
21. **Enrique II**, Rey de Castilla y de León, padre de
22. **Juan I**, Rey de Castilla y de León, padre de
23. **Enrique III**, Rey de Castilla y de León, padre de
24. **Juan II**, Rey de Castilla y de Leó, padre de
25. **Isabel I**, Reina de Castilla y de León, casada con Fernando II de Aragón, padres de
26. **Juana I** de España casada con Felipe de Austria, padres de
27. **Carlos I**, padre de
28. **Felipe II**, padre de
29. **Felipe III**, padre de
30. **Felipe IV**, padre de
31. **Maria Teresa**, Infanta de España, casada con Luis XIV de Francia, padres de
32. **Luis (de Borbón)**, Delfin de Francia, padre de
33. **Felipe V**, padre de
34. **Carlos III**, padre de
35. **Carlos IV**, padre de
36. **Fernando VII**, padre de
37. **Isabel II**, casada con el Infante Don Francisco de Asis de Borbón, padres de
38. **Alfonso XII**, padre de
39. **Alfonso XIII**, padre de
40. **Juan**, Conde de Barcelona, padre de
41. **Juan Carlos I**.

Fig. 6. Genealogy of the Spanish royal family. Established for twelve centuries it is the oldest-reigning monarchy in Europe. Reproduced by permission of *Diario ABC de Madrid*. *Padre de* = father of. *Padres de* = parents of. *Casada con* = married to. *Rey/Reina* = King/Queen. *Conde de* = Count of.

1981. In the autumn elections, the Socialist Party, headed by Felipe Gonzalez, enjoyed a landslide victory.

Socialist domination

The period after 1982 was marked by a substantial majority with a 'steam-roller' vote which ensured that the Government's wishes were obeyed and rubber-stamped by the Cortes (Parliament). The Socialist Party had maintained an internal discipline, permitting nobody to resign thus making for a stable government. Scandal after scandal was unearthed but public enquiries were never permitted and ministers remained at their posts.

During the 1980s many allegations were made against the brother of the Vice President of the Government. Juan Guerra was accused of using his influence and of being involved in numerous scandals. Each time Alfonso Guerra tendered his resignation and each time the President, Felipe González, refused to accept it.

In 1991, the formal legal proceedings against Juan Guerra began to show that there was truth in the allegations and that he had amassed a considerable private fortune during the period that the Socialists had been in power (as had many other). Alfonso Guerra immediately offered to resign again. This time his resignation was accepted and the powerful coalition broken between the President who governed and the Vice President who continued to control the Socialist Party.

This bi-partisan leadership helped greatly to keep the Socialist Party in power between 1980 and 1992. Its termination signalled the 'beginning of the end' of Socialist domination.

General elections of 1996

Change came in 1996, when finally the Opposition achieved the greatest number of votes. In fact, their majority depended on the small number of votes of the regional parties of the Basques, and Canary Islands' deputies. Their main aid was the Catalan votes.

There are periodic 'bickerings' between the main party, the PP or *Partido Popular*, and those regional ones. Such disputes usually die down after a few weeks, with fresh concessions being made to restore their very necessary co-operation against the opposition Socialist Party.

The *Financial Times* of 17 November 1997 dedicated a special issue to Spain, saying it has one of the best European economies, with a 'golden future' and outlook. The PP government has become firmly established, bringing down the cost of electricity and other commodities, reducing governmental costs, and implementing taxation reforms, all leading to a healthy growth in GNP, (4.2% growth in the year 2000).

Furthermore Aznar's government has kept free of scandals to date, thus strengthening the PP's hold on power. Stability and decency are pursued to ensure the greatest vote catching possible. In the same way, success in their fight against the ETA terrorist organisation brings further public backing to the PP Government.

PREDICTING THE POLITICAL FUTURE

A Chinese proverb states that if someone could know only one day in advance tomorrow's news, they could become a millionaire. While having no ambition in that direction, the evidence is that the PP party show themselves to be firmly entrenched with an absolute majority following the last General Election, their popularity is ascending instead of being reduced by the normal political wear and tear. So that for those considering business investments in the European Union, Spain is a favourite location.

3

Dealing with the Spanish

Whether the differences in Spain are purely idiosyncratic or are the result of past history, they must be acknowledged. Some people maintain that 'Spain is just another country in modern Europe' but even a brief stay or study of Spanish philology will reveal that this is untrue and that there is no sign that this will change.

The European Union has started to bring the country in line with the other member states but there is little sign of it actually happening. In spite of EU protests, progress remains slow.

Since this is the prevailing attitude, this chapter attempts to tell you how to cope with it.

USING THE POST OFFICE

Most Spanish post offices from La Coruña to Tenerife open from 09.00 until 14.30, five days a week (Saturdays, 09.00 to 13.00). Again according to EU plans, they should also be opening in the afternoons – but the old timetable continues, except for parcel collection which is now possible until 20.30 on weekdays.

The mysteries of the postal system – opening hours

Northern Europeans accustomed to drawing their pensions whenever they please will find that 'morning only' is the general rule. As mentioned, opening hours are 09.00 until 14.30 with no overtime. During this period, you can buy stamps, collect mail from an *apartado* (PO Box), send telegrams, use the Post Office Savings Bank (*Caja de Ahorros*) and a few other things. However, that being said, woe betide you if you attempt to register a letter after 13.00, buy a postal order, etc. In most post offices this can only be done until 13.00, after which you have to wait until the next day.

The larger cities have a more European timetable and most services are open in the evenings, when often queues form. This applies to Madrid's main GPO, in the Plaza de Cibeles and provincial capitals too.

Time is therefore restricted and the queues can make visiting the post office a time-consuming activity. If you have to collect a parcel, take a good book or use the time to brush up your Spanish as the queues may be very long. Standards have slipped back rapidly since Franco's time but the State has promised to make an investment of 200,000 million pesetas during the 1990s. Nevertheless the public has become so accustomed to promises that it will take a great deal of evidence to convince it.

There are fewer mysteries in the main cities and the capitals of the provinces. Many postal services are available from 09.00 until 22.00 or even midnight. You can check out registered letters in Madrid's GPO all day, as well as check them in. Postal services come near to the European norm although you will still have to stand in one queue to buy stamps, and another if you would like the clerk to make up your parcel and seal it. (This is a cheap and welcome service which ensures that parcels comply with regulations.) In some of the most popular tourist zones, multi-lingual staff may be available – but they are the exception.

Please remember that these details are general, and there may be regional variations. If you travel from one part of Spain to another and you have important first class mail, it is better to find out what facilities are available beforehand rather than assume it will be the same as where you have come from.

Letters

Incoming and outgoing mail may pose many problems to the newcomer to Spain. The delays in delivering mail in normal residential districts have to be experienced to be believed so it is well worth obtaining a post office box or *apartado (de correos)*. It may save days on letter delivery and means that you can receive your mail almost as soon as it arrives at the local post office. This applies particularly if you decide to 'live out in the sticks'. Getting a fax machine is an alternative method of staying 'in touch'.

Bulky parcels of printed matter or other material will not be delivered to the house in any case, unless you happen to live in a big city in which case you may pay a special fee.

If you think you may need an *apartado* ask yourself the following questions:

- Do I *need* to receive mail rapidly?

- Do I receive a lot of mail?

- Could postal delays affect my income?

- Do I intend to live in an isolated location?

- Do I wish to receive letters as soon as possible?

- Do I receive cheques in the post?

An *apartado* costs very little and once obtained needs to be renewed annually. Currently 2500 pesetas a year.

Posting letters is also a problem. In the past the express letter (*urgente*) has been the solution. It cost 70 pesetas to send an internal letter, 80 pesetas for an international, but those times are ending. For a time postal costs were pegged. Now the current express fee is 300 or more pesetas.

If your mail is not so urgent get into the habit of taking your mail to the nearest post office before 13.00. Although the official closing time is 14.30 most mailbags are sealed an hour earlier and normally only '*urgentes*' will catch the post after that time.

Special tips

- Use post boxes as little as possible and always mail from a post office.

- If you are anywhere near the main post office in a city or a town make use of its services.

- If you frequently have urgent mail to post it is worth going to the nearest airport which normally has a post office. Some indeed, have a special post office building well away from the terminals.

- Tipping used to be almost an obligation but is the exception these days. However, it is well worth cultivating the staff you deal with. A Christmas tip will be remembered all year and may even help cut out some of the queuing if you become a regular.

- Using the postal code will also help you to keep on good terms with the staff of *Correos* (Post Office) even if at times they seem to ignore it. The Post Office publishes a guide to postal codes, the *Guía Codigo Postal*, which lists each street in cities down to house numbers in small villages and hamlets. It is worth remembering that *apartado* codes end in 80, e.g. Apartado 14,762, 28080 Madrid. (This is the author's address.)

- Anyone who lives near the Rock of Gibraltar will tell you to post your letters in Gibraltar, if they are bound for Britain or the Rock. Vice versa also applies, so the Gibraltarians cross the frontier to use *Correos* for mail with a Spanish destination. The delays are considerable otherwise and it can take a month for mail to cross the frontier. It seems that *Correos* still remembers the time when the frontier was closed and people and mail had to travel via Tangier to and from the Rock. The special Gibraltar stamps are an added incentive to use the post office there.

TELECOMMUNICATIONS

The state of Spanish telecommunications has been transformed during the last five years. The Cia. Telefónica has lost its age-old monopoly, with great benefits for the public. So phone tariffs have at last moved downwards, and Telefónica has introduced free offers and other incentives to use their services. Their chief rival at first was the Airtel company, which began with mobile telephones and rapidly offered 95% coverage of national territory. For many months mobile phones were offered 'for free', which seemed ideal – until the bills came in, when it became clear they would soon recover any loss.

Telefónica joined battle, and thus mobile phones for all became the order of the day in Spain – they appear *everywhere* nowadays.

Then at the end of 1997 came the blow, with mobile tariffs increased by as much as 20 per cent. That followed sales of two million mobiles in the first eight months of 1997. But this has not discouraged the public. A study by Coopers & Lybrand predicts the total number of mobile phones will be some 30 million by the year 2017, meaning every person between 10 and 70 years old should have one. Results were 'satisfactory' with Telefónica Móviles reporting sales of 264,084 mpts (=million pesetas), 47.8 per cent more than the first nine months of 1997/96. Profits were 15,475 mpts. Respective figures for Airtel for all 1997 were 110,000 mpts sales and profits of some 15,000 mpts.

A third operator was scheduled to join the fight for the start of 1998. This has resulted in still lower tariffs and more benefits for the public. By the end of this year, there should be 4.2 million mobiles in Spain; by the end of 2000, 8 million; by the end of 2002, 10 million. So living and working in Spain will be easier with this facility, so well installed. However, many business users are locking away their mobiles, because of the high cost of usage. But Telefónica Móviles SA attack again, with suggestions for effecting great savings in their usage, including the installation of their Movi Star Enlace phone exchange (just dial 123).

Everyday phone usage

The popularity of mobile phones means that long delays in getting a phone installed are now a thing of the past. Within twenty-four hours, almost any one can have an operational mobile. Telefónica says they install a stationary phone within fifiteen days; but with three operators, that period and conditions should soon be improved for clients (just dial 004).

Those three operators will soon have to meet a bill of 50,000 mpts as a result of one of the latest decisions of the Council of Ministers. This is the change in numeration implemented on 4 April 1998. Now it is necessary to use a prefix, e.g. 91 for Madrid, 952 for Málaga, etc., for all national calls and not only inter-provincial calls as previously. This will permit expansion from 100 million to 1,000 million phone numbers – sufficient for three operators . . . and more. To phone abroad, you should now use 00 as in the UK . . . more moves towards EU standardisation. So to dial UK, use 00 – 44 – etc. To dial Spain from the UK, use 00 – 34 – etc.

This new system was introduced to permit new operators to function, with Retevisión having begun on 1 January 1998 and others following. The aim is to give customers a wide choice and much lower costs than previously, when telecommunications were very expensive, and the profits of Cia. Telefónica very high.

Finding and using public phones

Suppose you are travelling off the beaten track. How can you make a phone call? It can be difficult to find a public telephone let alone a working telephone, and even then it may be in a noisy bar. This is what you should do.

- Find a decent hotel. You will be able to make your call in peace and quiet. It will, of course, cost a little more and a tip will be expected.

- Find one of the better restaurants or cafés. The same will apply as above.

- If you are in a city, look for a shop in the *Corte Inglés* chain or a department store. They normally have public telephones available.

- The offices of officialdom often have a public telephone hidden away.

- You can make long distance calls and reverse charges calls from any *Telefónica* office.

There are exceptions, of course. You may make calls from main post offices, but not from small post offices.

Fax
The use of fax is popular, as with mobile phones. Nowadays most newsagents, photocopying shops, have a fax installed for international etc. and national usages, both to receive and to send at a reasonable cost. If you prefer, you can attach a fax unit to your phone line, and use it together. Fax is also available from main post offices but is more expensive there than in shops.

The Spanish have traditionally hated the use of mail, but adapt well to fax with its immediate reception as with the phone.

Telex
Utilisation of telex is at a low ebb. Although it is still possible to send from main post offices, it is often difficult. Only the largest concerns and companies use it normally, as nearly all have changed over to fax usage, which is quicker and more convenient in many ways. Obviously a lot of people now use email.

Telegrams
This is one service you will find in most post offices but it is only available in the mornings when these establishments are open. During the rest of the day you may phone telegrams in. You are unlikely to find an English speaking telephone clerk, however, unless you are in the Costa Blanca or the Islands.

Some negative aspects
As post offices are open for so short a time you can buy stamps in normal shop hours from those shops officially licensed to sell tobacco, but not from the many other unofficial outlets for the weed. Always check your change carefully!

Several years ago the EEC opined that post offices should have longer opening hours, but the traditional ways linger on. The hope was also expressed that services offered should at least begin to approach those available in the rest of Europe – but there it rests!

In the meantime the delivery of mail may take a very long time, staff may be unhelpful and unwilling even to try to understand a different language, let alone speak it. Complaints, when made, rarely have any effect.

If you receive bad service ask for the *hoja de reclamaciones* (official complaints form). Normally the mere threat will be efficient to settle matters but if you are intending to use the service regularly it is better to stop short of the actual deed.

WORKING HOURS AND HOLIDAYS

Banks
These have very similar opening hours to post offices. In summer, however, they may be closed on Saturday mornings. The savings banks (*cajas*) are closed on Saturday mornings throughout the year but stay open on Thursday afternoons.

The Administration
'*Nadie ama a su patria porque sea grande, sino porque es suyo*'. Seneca. (Nobody loves his fatherland because it is large, only because it is his.)

This sums up the attitude of many officials, especially when dealing with foreigners. It was especially prevalent in Franco's regime and still exists to some extent even now. One favourite tactic is to make you queue. You may spend a very long time in one queue only to find you have been directed to the wrong queue and should have been waiting in the next one . . . and so on. *Persistence* is essential when dealing with the Administration and the one weapon which really pays off. The battle will be won when the Administration is made to realise that you are not going to give up.

As usual, there are exceptions. On the Costa del Sol, and the other areas where the influx of hundreds of thousands of foreign residents has raised the standard of living so considerably, you may expect better treatment. Just remember that in Spain a civil servant is not necessarily civil nor a servant.

Working hours

Offices are officially open to the public from 09.00 or 10.00 until 14.00. In practice this may be a little different. Spaniards are not noted for their punctuality so they may not arrive at work on time. Then it is the custom to have a cup of coffee. In this way opening hours may be curtailed.

In the Ministries the staff are supposed to work in the afternoons but if you telephone during this period you are likely to be told, '*Señor Tal y Tal* (So and So) is not back from lunch yet,' until about 18.00 when it will change to: 'It seems that *Señor Tal y Tal* will not be back this afternoon, you had better 'phone tomorrow morning'. If you are very lucky you will catch up with your *señor* somewhere in his arduous timetable and make an appointment which should be checked again before arriving at the agreed meeting place.

Business hours

An infinite variety of office hours are to be found in Spain and any business traveller is well advised to find out in advance what office hours are kept by the firms he intends to visit. If this is not done a considerable amount of time may be wasted in fruitless visits going from one closed office to another.

The traditional working hours are 09.30 until 13.30 and 16.30 until 19.30, thus allowing a *siesta*. Nowadays there is a trend towards reducing the lunch break and finishing earlier. Multinationals, however, may insist on imposing Stateside or British working hours. Staff comment, 'We can make hardly any external contacts in the afternoons.'

In the hottest summer months Spanish companies may adopt the *horario intensivo* (non-stop timetable). This is popular with staff even though it means officially working non-stop from 08.00 or 09.00 until 15.00, five days a week. This leaves staff free to spend the afternoon in the swimming pool, or have a siesta, as well as giving them a free weekend. (In winter, banks and a surprising number of concerns work on Saturday mornings.) It should be said, however, that the *horario intensivo* very often includes a meal break and the inevitable morning coffee.

Some companies too are introducing flexible working hours.

Other variations

Another variable to be considered is the great regional difference in Spain, from the deserts in the Canary Islands and province of

Almería, to the vegetation and climatic conditions of the north which can be similar to the British Isles. Due to the wide scope of Spain's climate and geography, you will find business working hours are affected.

Business lunches in Spain

The Spanish business lunch is one reason why an international survey states that Spanish executives waste about 40 per cent of their time. They will meet at a four or five fork restaurant at about 14.00 and continue until 17.00 and later, and discuss business amongst many other topics. They may consume a four or five course meal and refuse dessert in favour of a strong coffee to fight off sleep and, perhaps, clinch the deal.

Business trips

Spaniards like to show lavish hospitality. Any business trip for the top flight may include five star hotels and restaurants. Dinners may extend well into the small hours of the morning yet everyone will be bright and alert for a 07.00 start. Many Spaniards seem to be able to survive several days of this pace, with no apparent need for sleep – just a lot of black coffee. So if you are planning a business trip to Spain, you should arrive well rested and prepared for a strenuous time during which luxury meals may well alternate with factory and plant visits with little time for sleep.

Shopping hours

Those long Spanish shopping hours can fill your evenings if you are an enthusiast for *compras* (buys). The main department stores open from 10.00 until 20.00. Hypermarkets open from 10.00 until 22.00 and on a few Sunday mornings. The average shop will open from 09.00 until 20.00, closing for two to three hours around midday, and even longer when the great heat arrives in summer. These hours are the norm, subject to the usual regional variations.

It is extremely convenient to be able to shop whenever you like in the same way as you can find somewhere to eat or drink. Once you become accustomed to these opening hours it becomes positively irksome to return to northern Europe and find everything closed so much earlier. This is definitely one of Spain's good points and there is no change in sight.

Shopping outlets are supplemented by the street markets usually held once a week. On this day the town will be closed to traffic and the shoppers throng from 08.00 until 14.00. The market is a colourful event and ranges in character from the cosmopolitan atmosphere of the one in Javea (Alicante) to the typical rural *mercado* in Asturias where bargains are still to be found.

When you go shopping, please remember the following advice. It will save you a lot of trouble and expense:

- If you can, take a Spanish friend with you; if not, choose a shop where the prices are clearly marked.

- Shop around for the best bargain.

- If you need to replace anything, especially lightbulbs, it is always best to take the old one with you.

- Never forget to check your change, even when you have been a regular client for years.

- Keep a sharp eye on your money, credit cards, briefcase, shopping trolley, etc., etc. – all can disappear rapidly!

Public holidays

These are a perfect example of clinging to established habits. Easter sees a massive yearly exodus, often to the same place. Christmas finds all at home eating roast lamb and *besugo* (sea bream) on Christmas Eve, a centuries old custom. New Year's Eve requires the provision of grapes. If you are to be lucky in the coming year you must eat a grape at each stroke of midnight. These customs are similar to many others around the world but the Spaniard is a great enthusiast for a public holiday. Here is a list of the national holidays. Those marked* may be replaced by the autonomous regions for other celebrations.

New Year's Day	1 January
The Holy Kings' Day*	6 January
St Joseph's Day*	19 March
Holy Thursday*	
Good Friday*	
Labour Day	1 May
Ascension Day	
St James' Day*	25 July
National Holiday	12 October
All Saints Day	1 November
Constitution Day	6 December

Immaculate Conception Day	8 December
Christmas Day	25 December

All holidays/fiestas which fall on a Sunday are changed to have the following Monday off.

Puentes (bridges) and *viaductos* (viaducts) are famous and often condemned but are still celebrated. A *puente* occurs when a holiday falls on a Tuesday or Thursday. Most people will also take Monday or Friday off as well to make a long weekend. Only a few unfortunates in banks or the odd office or factory where it has not been allowed will still be in work. *Puentes* are a way of life for the majority which cost industry billions every year. *Viaductos* are even better – or worse if you are an employer. These occur when a regional *fiesta* adjoins a national holiday; for example, 1 May is a national holiday and 2 May a regional holiday in the province of Madrid. When these two holidays fall midweek people usually take the rest of the week off.

Regional holidays

In addition to all the national public holidays each of Spain's seventeen regions has its own *fiesta* and every town and village has another day for its own *fiesta*. Whenever the government tries to reduce the number of *fiestas* there is such a public outcry that the threat is never carried out. This permissiveness is doubtless a vote-catcher. In Spain obtaining votes has the same importance as a sacred rite in a pagan religion and the Spanish also take their holidays and *fiestas* very seriously.

Holiday shutdowns

Thus business visitors should make a check on holiday dates before embarking on any trip. Working hours are curtailed even more during main holiday periods. Spain virtually closes down during August, except for the main tourist zones. The inland cities and towns are virtually empty and it is easy to park the car. However many establishments will be closed and you may have a long walk just to buy a morning newspaper. Normal business contacts will be impossible as all those in positions of responsibility will be on holiday. It is also a very bad time of the year to fall ill and need hospital treatment.

Apart from the month of August itself 'anyone who is anyone' will disappear from the office between mid-July and mid-September. Business visits should be avoided during this period.

Occasionally some Minister will give great publicity to the fact that it is his intention to work during August.

The same applies to the period between mid-December and mid-January. Since the official public holidays are 24 and 25 December and 1 and 6 January it makes a convenient time for the executive to enjoy a skiing break. The Catalans have another *fiesta* during this period, 26 December.

In Spain continuing work during the periods mentioned becomes almost impossible. Some multinationals have tried to alter the pattern but with little success. Any attempt to make the Spanish way of life conform to the European norm usually has as much success as King Canute with his oceanographic experiments.

DOCUMENTATION FOR RESIDENCE PURPOSES

'You do *not* need a work permit now, and you have every right to a residence card as an EU citizen,' assures one of the UK Consulate officials in one of the fifteen UK Consulates in Spanish territory. So finally EU rules and regulations are being applied in Spain, after 'many moons'.

However, consulates also warn repeatedly that for OAPs from the UK, DSS benefits are not sufficient to cover the costs of a couple living in Spain. Many have found this out for themselves, rather painfully, and have had to return to the UK. However, those with a private income, or other means, which can be shown to the Spanish authorities, are made most welcome.

Residence cards

After staying longer than six months in Spain, you must apply for a residence card, at the local Comisarí de Policía or in Madrid at Comisario de Tetuán, Plaza de la Remonta, Pasaje Maestros Ladrilletos s/n Madrid (near Metro: Valdeacederas). Tel: 91 571 92 00. Freephone: 900 15 00 00 00. Open: 09.00 to 14.00 hours weekdays. Your application must be accompanied by:

- job contract or certificate from your employer

- three passport-sized colour photos

- valid passport and photocopies of its pages.

Documents for the self-employed

Self-employed persons must establish that they have applied for all necessary documentation to engage in their proposed activity and proved that they have sufficient funds. That would be the same as required from any Spanish citizen in the same circumstances. The Spanish are well accustomed to such complex procedures when dealing with their Administration. It may be necessary to employ a *gestor* (a person who specialises in dealing with paperwork) to ensure the documents are complete and correct:

1. *Solicitud Licencia de Apertura del Ayuntamiento* = application for Opening Licence from the Town Hall/Council.
2. *Solicitud Licencia Municipal* = application for the Municipal licence.
3. *Solicitud de Apertura de la Dirección Territorial de Trabajo y Sanidad y Seguridad Social* = application for the opening from the Territorial Directorate of Empoyment, Health and Social Security.
4. *Alta como Autónomo en la Seguridad Social* = certificate of enrolment as self-employed in the Social Security.
5. *Alta Licencia Fiscal* = business licence.
6. *Solicitud Autorización de la Consejería de Turismo y Transportes* = application for authorisation from the Council of Transport and Tourism.
7. *Concesión de la Jefatura de Costas* = authorisation from the coastal authorities (if on one of the Costas).
8. *Solicitud Autorización de Manipuladores de Alimentación* = application for food handling authorisation.
9. *Solicitud Autorización del Ministerio de Transportes, Turismo y Comunicaciónes* = application for authorization from the Ministerio de Fomento.
10. Proof of professional/educational qualifications recognised under Spanish/EU legislation.

4

Buying Property in Spain

CHOOSING WHERE TO LIVE

Spain is not like Chile, a long thin strip of land between the sea and the mountain ranges, and yet publicity has restricted the knowledge of millions of visitors to this topography. Spanish territory includes fascinating mountain regions with peaks of 3,000 metres, vast pine forests and every kind of terrain. So if you are considering a retirement home in Spain it is worthwhile giving some thought to the other possibilities before you automatically decide on a coastal region. After all, in Britain some people retire to the Cotswolds as well as to Sussex or Cornwall.

Some points to ponder

It is worth considering whether your dream home is to be used as a permanent residence or a holiday home as well as deciding on its ideal characteristics.

If you need to know the climatic conditions of the seventeen regions of Spain you can write to the appropriate tourist office. It will detail with joy the large number of hours of sunshine but seldom mention very important features like the humidity.

Generally, however, you should get out your map of Spain and ask yourself a few questions like the following:

- Exactly which type of climate would I most enjoy? Central Spain would be very suitable if you prefer a dry climate with very hot summers and cold winters.

- What are the advantages and disadvantages for me of living near the sea? High humidity in summer can be very trying.

- Could I adapt to an island life? If so, the Balearics or the Canaries are obvious choices. Remember, however, that the Canaries are as far from Madrid as London and Majorca's airport is very crowded during the peak summer season.

- Is the allure of day after day of cloudless skies strong enough? It can become boring, believe it or not! It also restricts the conversation.

- Where do other people live? According to the World Health Organisation, Javea on the Costa Blanca is the ideal. Statistics show a greater number of GB registered plates here than anywhere else in Spain.

These are just a few points to start you thinking, but whichever of the seventeen regions you choose, you will normally find a warm welcome there. As you can see on the map, page 10, the land mass is important. The mainland covers 491,205 square kms, and the island groups, 12,286 square kms. If you have a Greta Garbo complex and just like to be alone, then the sparsely populated wide open spaces of Spain's interior could be ideal for you. At the opposite extreme, those with a 'sardine tin' complex would be very happy on the beaches of Benidorm, Tossa de Mar or even those in the northern province of Santander. These northern beaches are becoming more popular now with the Spanish and foreigners as global warming continues to affect the climate.

Useful addresses

It can be very useful to write for information to those regions in which you are specially interested supplied in English or other language of your choice.

If you are intending to invest in Spain and/or establish anything from a small firm to a large company, the regional Minister of Industry would be delighted to hear from you. Many incentives are offered to foreign investors. Address your letter to the *Consejero de Comercio e Industria* followed by the address of the regional government in question. Each regional government has its own Council of Ministers (*Consejeros*) and civil service. Thus it can be no surprise to learn that there are now 2.4 million civil servants in Spain, counting all those employed by central, regional and municipal administrations.

The following list of addresses gives the name of the *comunidad autónoma* (autonomous region) first, followed by the title of its government and the address.

Comunidad Autónoma de Andalucía, Junta de Andalucía, Palacio de San Telmo Avda, de Roma s/n, 41071, Seville. Tel: 95 459 75 00. Fax: 95 459 75 94. Telex: 72854.

Comunidad Autónoma de Aragón, Diputación de Aragón, Paseo María Agustin 36, 50071 Zaragoza. Tel: 976 71 40 00. Fax: 976 71 41 81. Telex: 58008.

Comunidad Autónoma de Cantabria, (formerly Santander) *Diputación Regional de Cantabria*, calle Casimiro Sainz 4, 39003 Santander (Cantabria). Tel: 942 20 71 02. Fax: 942 20 72 14.

Comunidad Autónoma de Castilla–La Mancha, Junta de Comunidades de Castilla–La Mancha, Palacio de Fuensalida, Plaza de Conde 2, 45002 Toledo. Tel: 925 26 76 00. Fax: 925 26 76 05. Telex: 47995.

Comunidad Autónoma de Castilla y León, Junta de Castilla y León, Pza. de Castilla y Léon, 47006 Valladolid. Tel: 983 41 11 00. Fax: 983 47 32 54. Telex: 26567.

Comunidad Autónoma de Cataluña, Generalitat de Cataluña, Palau de la Generalitat, Plaza de San Jaime s/n, 08002 Barcelona (Cataluña). Tel: 93 402 46 00 and 93 402 48 00. Fax: 93 302 63 45. Telex: 51545.

Comunidad Autónoma de Extremadura, Junta de Extremadura, calle Jose Fernandez Lopez 18, 06800 Merida (Badajoz). Tel: 924 38 14 38 and 924 38 11 38. Fax: 924 38 14 59/53.

Comunidad Autónoma de Galicia, Junta de Galicia, Palacio de Rojoy, 15705 Santiago de Compostela (La Coruña). Tel: 981 54 54 00. Fax: 981 54 12 19. Telex: 88097.

Comunidad Autónoma de las Islas Balaeres, Gobierno de las Islas Balaeres, calle Marina 3 – Consulado del Mar, 07012 Palma de Mallorca (Mallorca). Tel: 971 17 65 65. Fax: 971 17 65 87.

Comunidad Autónoma de las Islas Canarias, Gobierno Canario, Plaza 25 de Julio 1, 35004 Las Palmas de Gran Canaria (Islas Canarias). Tel: 928 45 21 00. Fax: 928 45 21 43/50.

Comunidad Autónoma de Madrid, Gobierno de la Comunidad de Madrid, Puerta del Sol 7, 28013 Madrid. Tel: 91 580 15 92 and 91 580 15 87/93/94. Fax: 91 580 20 68.

Comunidad Autónoma del País Vasco, Gobierno Vasco, (Basque Government) Palacio de Ajuna-Enea, 01007 Vitoria (Alava). Tel: 945 18 79 00. Fax: 945 18 78 32. Telex: 35463.

Comunidad Autónoma de La Rioja, Consejo de Gobierno de La Rioja, calle General Vara del Rey 3, 26071, Logroño. Tel: 941 29 11 00 and 941 29 11 08. Fax: 941 29 12 71.

Comunidad Autónoma de Valencia, Generalidad Valenciana, Palau de la Generalitat, 46003 Valencia. Tel: 96 386 61 00. Fax: 96 391 25 33. Telex: 63071.

Comunidad Floral de Navarra, Diputación Floral de Navarra, 1, 31002 Pamplona (Navarra). Tel: 948 42 70 00. Fax: 948 22 76 73. Telex: 37817.

Principado de Asturias, Consejo de Gobierno del Principado de Asturias, calle Suárez de la Riva, 33071 Oviedo (Asturias). Tel: 985 10 67 66. Fax: 985 10 67 65.

Región de Murcia, Consejo de Gobierno de Murcia, Palacio de San Esteban, calle Acisco Diaz s/n, 30071 Murcia. Tel: 968 36 20 00 and 968 29 40 11. Fax: 968 29 30 75. Telex: 67641.

Ceuta, Consejo de Gobierno Ciudad Autonoma, Pza. Africa s/n, 51001 Ceuta. Tel: 956 52 82 00/25. Fax: 956 51 44 70.

Melilla, Consejo de Gobierno Cuidad Autonoma, 52001 Melilla. Tel: 95 268 16 63 and 95 269 91 38. Fax: 95 267 48 00.

You could also try writing to the appropriate *Oficina de Turismo* or, if you prefer to impress, the *Consejero de Turismo* (Minister of Tourism). In some cases like the *Consejería de Turismo y Transportes* of the Canaries, and the *Junta de Extremadura* you will receive an attractive book which will give you plenty of information.

Reading the weekly English newspaper *Sur in English* will put you into the picture about all facets of life on the Costa del Sol, from clubs and scandal, to news and sport. Every winter there is a competition. The 25 winning couples are taken on a tour of Andalucía, enjoying luxury hotels and restaurants. If you are lucky enough to win, as we were, you will enjoy the experience. They also publish lists of numerous clubs, and main meeting places of 15 religions, including Muslims, Jews, Jehovah's Witnesses, etc.

The Canaries

The Canary Islands are the choice of many foreigners for a holiday home or something more permanent. The seven main islands and four smaller ones cover 7,501 square kms. They are 1,100 kms from Cádiz and are a mere 115 km from Fuerteventura to Cape Juby in Africa. Thus the climate and general appearance owe more to Africa than Europe. If you like the heat, year-round swimming and sunbathing – there are many naturist beaches – then the Canaries could be for you.

The tourist books talk of a privileged climate. This means that they have a year-round season. The main flow of national visitors comes during the summer, and during the winter the Scandinavians flee here from their winter black-out.

However, a stay on the islands is essential before you finally decide. Conversations with the locals may save you much expense. For example, although the guidebooks extol the constant warm climate the taxi drivers will tell you a slightly different story. 'When the *calima* blows in from Africa, the heat and humidity become insupportable. Water shortages are frequent, together with serious drought periods which can be lengthy.' The *calima* is a wind that blows in from Africa bearing sand from the Sahara.

Final advice

It is also a good idea to consider your chosen residence from the angle of winter as well as summer. A desirable residence in summer could turn out to have a leaky roof which drips water onto the beds. The unmade road leading up to it could become a quagmire in the winter rains. This applies everywhere throughout Spain.

You should also spend some time in the region and town of your choice. Perhaps you could rent a property there for a year, or several months at least before you take any practical steps towards a final move. When you have done all this you should have a clear idea of all its advantages and disadvantages.

There are in fact very few places to rent in Spain. Most people are owner-occupiers. When you do find a property to rent you should insist on a rent agreement.

TYPES OF PROPERTY AVAILABLE

The choice is enormous and ranges from the luxury villas of the millionaires on the Costa del Sol, Majorca and Costa Brava, to modest flats on the coasts of Valencia or Murcia where bargains may still be found.

Retirement homes

Catering for the retired and elderly is becoming big business in Spain as typified by the development called Almond Court at Muchamiel just 8 kms north of Alicante and 5 kms from its famous San Juan beach.

Phase One is mostly sold, Phase Two is now complete and Phases Three and Four will follow. It is an *urbanización* aimed at the retired. Many retired people from northern Europe are tempted here by the climate which offers 300 days of sunshine a year. The Manager at Almond Court, Senor Jorge Zanoletty Larrea, told me:

'About 70 per cent of our residents are British, followed by Dutch, Austrians, Italians, down to one German lady. We have designed everything for retired people, from a walk-down ramp in the swimming pool, to a resident doctor and nurse, 24-hour emergency alarm service with call cords in each flat. As the third age reaches ninety and beyond, we cater for all their needs.

'We believe that smaller flats are better so these range from 45 to 90 square metres in the first phase, and in the second almost all from 60 to 80 square metres on average, with just one type of 126 square metres. In the second phase, the promotion prices are 7.9 million pesetas for a single-bedroom flat, and from 10.5 million pesetas for a two-bedroom unit. The location is only about 50 metres from the town centre, so near banks, restaurants, and in the mainstream – different from many *residencias* for old people in Spain which are isolated in the countryside. For every metre of living space we sell in a private flat there is another metre provided in community services with a social club, library, gymnasium, pool, washing machine area, and so on, including a restaurant and cafeteria. We also provide a meals service to the flats and numerous other details.'

The company which runs this scheme is known as *Inter-Spain SA*. It is 25 per cent owned by one of the main bank groups, BBV (*Banco Bilbao Vizcaya*), having a capital of 163 million pesetas. Other banks which give references are: *Banco de Alicante, Banco de Comercio* and the savings bank known as the *Caja de Ahorros de Valencia*. The entire project consists of 200 flats and apartments and the first phase was inaugurated on 15 November 1989. Phase Two includes a small 24-room hotel for visiting relatives.

If you wish to buy one of the Almond Court development, you will usually have to pay 20 per cent of the total fee when you sign the contract, 20 per cent in monthly payments until completion of the building and the remainder when construction is finished, but other loans are available. The Spanish equivalent of VAT, IVA, is payable on top of the purchase price.

The Almond Court scheme is interesting because it follows the example of many Stateside developments for older residents, and its services are likely to be extended. Phase Three is for more flats and apartments but Phase Four will be a nursing home for the elderly who require full-time attention.

The Fisherman's Village
This is a more common development in all areas of Spain. It is exemplified by *La Alcazaba de Mijas*. This consists of offices, apartments and shops built in Mediterranean style and copying a fisherman's village, a welcome change from some of the horrible block developments which have ruined so much of the Spanish coastline. Similar attractive developments can be seen in Puerto de Mazarrón (Murcia), Javea (Alicante), the Costa Brava, and other Costas with many interesting offers.

Luxury accommodation
For sun worshippers the Roca Llisa development on Ibiza is typical of many. Luxury houses are built into the rocks beside the sea. It lies between Santa Eulalia and Ibiza city and covers 200 hectares with a golf course and all amenities.

Some housing developments are constructed alongside or within golf courses, some apartments in marinas and there are other speciality complexes.

BUILDING STANDARDS

The standard of finished buildings in Spain is as variable as topography and Spanish geography. If you decide to buy a new property through a foreign company the guarantee is usually good. The same applies to a luxury villa in an *urbanización* in Javea or near Denia. But if you have found a cut-price bargain flat in Almeria on the Costa de la Luz, or in some *pueblo* in the *Comunidad Valenciana* then you should exercise extreme caution.

Doubtless as time passes EU rules and regulations will come into effect. For the moment the motto is, as with so many matters, 'money arranges everything'. If you buy a quality product it will probably work out cheapest in the end. The bargain priced properties may cost large amounts to bring up to standard and your attempts to obtain satisfaction under the guarantee doomed to failure since the legal system is so slow that the builder will have disappeared by the time your case comes to court.

The best builders
In some areas with a large foreign population the state of the building art has been bettered, usually by foreign builders who have moved in. The product will be guaranteed to British Standards, DIN, or other regulations. For the newcomer to Spain there is a lot to be said for dealing with these builders. Not only is the language barrier ruled out, but such simple matters as kitchen table heights, mirror positions, storage space and the like are provided without having to embark on lengthy explanations. In Javea (Alicante) Taylor is a well-known builder and Country Properties of Competa (Málaga) offer town houses, villas and others from three million pesetas upwards. Advertisements on the Costa del Sol frequently mention 'creative building services', 'German Masterbuilder', 'ITS' (International Technical Services) and so on.

On the spot
However, as stated before, there really is no substitute for local knowledge which is impossible to include in any book in detail. This can only be obtained by talking to people. They have the experience and the latest information which can be invaluable to you. A visit to a restaurant, cafe, bar or even a park may offer a golden opportunity to start a conversation on the subject closest to your heart, a property. Do not make your decision on the basis

of one or two contacts or the over-friendly types who try to take you under their wing. When you have spoken to a dozen or score of people on the same subject and obtained a consensus of opinion, then you can come near to the truth.

The top-floor flat

Well over half the Spanish population lives in those large blocks of flats, apartments and duplex which are visible in all parts of Spanish territory from the population centres of the Canaries to Aragón, Galicia and Almería. Common complaints are about the neighbour who arrives home in the small hours of the morning, the children who live in the flat above and who ruin your *siesta* and a long line of other all too common complaints.

Thus the choice of a top-floor flat seems obvious. But if you do buy one, please check the roof. If not, you could wake up in the middle of the night with as close an acquaintance with rainwater as Gene Kelly in his dancing years. You, however, will not be dancing with joy, but possibly with rage. The charming salesman who assured you that the roof was completely rain-proof will have moved on and you will be faced with a long fight to get the builder to waterproof the domestic cupola. Our battle lasted five years and we only achieved this through pure persistence.

The law requires the builder to issue a full guarantee of his work for the ten-year period following construction but if it had not been for a constant barrage of letters, telephone calls, personal visits, registered letters, threats of legal action and general denunciation, we should have lost. Sheer persistence is a quality which pays off in Spain.

Of course, this is why many Spanish prefer a lower level flat or apartment. At the end of the 1990s, in fact, the tendency is to move to a house with a garden – however small it may be – even to tiny terraced houses.

NARROWING THE CHOICE

When you have decided roughly where you would like to live and what sort of property you would like to buy you should ask all those questions you would normally pose when buying property in any other country.

Is a motorway scheduled for the area? Is there any risk of a disco being installed nearby? These and many other questions may be resolved by paying a visit to the Town Hall (*Ayuntamiento*). As usual this may be time-consuming so arm yourself with a good book and a Spanish-speaking acquaintance – except in the areas where foreigners are common. You may prefer to instruct your *abogado* (lawyer) to do this.

It is also a good idea to find out whether the local amenities are seasonal or available all year round. It might also be worth considering a property 'facing' the sun. Great heat savings may be made in winter.

You should also check the general condition of the property, especially if it is not new. Since rainfall may be rare in some areas of Spain under normal conditions, the assumption is often made that rain will never fall. You may see proof of this in the largest cities which flood regularly when there is a mere half hour of heavy rain, causing immediate chaos and traffic jams.

Thus you ought to check that there is a damp-proof course (they are not always considered necessary). Floors may also be laid on bare soil and sewerage facilities should be checked in older properties.

You will meet many high-pressure salesmen in your property-buying efforts. Some will offer free flights from London and entertainment of various sorts. You should *never* sign any document when you deal with these types. Look for the 'soft sell' approach. It is often the sign of a quality product.

Nowadays it is very much a buyers' market so you may safely ignore such threats as, 'This is the last flat of this type that we have' and, 'It's the only house available in this area'. Today there is a wide choice of every type and size of property, and some bargains can be found given time and effort.

PURCHASE AND THE LAW

Once you have chosen your property, you should check its title since there are one or two nasty possibilities. Alternatively your *abogado* (lawyer) could do this.

- Registration. If you are buying a new property the builder will have to register it at the *Ayuntamiento*. This should be checked. Alternatively the registration of an older property should be checked against the *Registro de Propriedad* (property registry). If your intended property has no deeds, one of your first expenses may be to have the deeds drawn up which can be very costly.

- Tax arrears. If the owner has not paid certain taxes, the law allows a charge to be placed on the property. This will be recorded on the title. If you purchase such a property you will become liable for the arrears. The same applies when buying a second-hand car – you would be liable for any outstanding fines, or annual car tax payments which may be outstanding. This system is enforced for any property sale from a motor cycle to a luxury mansion.

- It is perfectly legal in Spain for a builder or property owner to take out a mortgage (*hipoteca*) on the property you are interested in while you are negotiating its purchase or even after you have done so. If this occurs, you, again, will find yourself liable to repay the loan, as has happened to many unwary buyers.

The Property Register (Registro de Propriedad)
Transfer of property ownership should always be registered though as usual in Spain this does not always occur. If there is any doubt about ownership it is wiser to abandon the purchase than engage in legal battles. However, in normal cases you will find this register useful because it will inform you whether the property has been registered, whether there are arrears of taxes or an outstanding mortgage, whether an agency or company is involved. It can be very complicated in the case of the latter.

The Property Register should be inspected twice. You should check it at the start of the purchase and again at the end just before you register your ownership of the property and complete the purchase.

The legal process
Once you have done all this and transferred the purchase money into a Spanish bank in internal pesetas you will be ready to sign the conveyancing document (*escritura de compraventa*). No conveyance is legal or binding unless it has been signed in the presence of a notary. The notary will want to see a certificate from your bank to confirm that the purchase money has come from abroad and a copy of form TE 13, submitted to the Ministry of Commerce with the details of the purchase, approved with the official stamp.

Please bear in mind that the *escritura* is the only document which will guarantee your title. Any other kind of deed or contract you may be persuaded to sign will have little effect. Any legal redress may be a very, very long time coming.

Once the conveyance has been signed it should be sent to the *Registro de Propriedad* to be registered. Once this has been done (and in some areas it may take up to a year) your title becomes final.

The legal process described applies as much to the city as to the country and should be followed through carefully. The Spanish legal system is largely inoperative due to delays of many years and the *Tribunal Supreme* (Supreme Court) has a backlog of thirty-five thousand cases. Local courts may take five or ten years to get round to an average case. If you do not have a local to intervene, you might seriously have to take your life expectancy into account when contemplating legal action.

On the other hand, many thousands of foreigners have bought properties in Spain, followed all the legal processes and have had no problems whatsoever.

USING PROFESSIONAL ADVISERS

The Abogado
This man is a lawyer. You will employ him to safeguard your interests. This means that you must check that your chosen *abogado* is not already working for your vendor. It is quite legal for an *abogado* to do this, but it is obvious that there may be a conflict of interest. An *abogado* will give you advice, and take care of the legal aspects of buying a property. Needless to say he should be reliable. Some addresses are given at the back of this book.

The Notary
This man is a public official for whom there is no British equivalent. His duty is to ensure that legal transactions are carried out correctly. He has no interest in either party; he will neither act for you nor protect you.

The Gestor

You will obtain the services of a *gestor* from a *gestoria*. Again he has no British equivalent. He deals with all kinds of paperwork, licences, permits, taxation etc.

ADDITIONAL EXPENSES

You may expect the following additional expenses on top of the purchase.

Tax on the transaction

If you are buying an older property you will have to pay 5½ per cent transfer tax *(impuesto sobre transmisiones)*. If you are buying from a developer you will have to pay 12 per cent IVA (the equivalent of VAT) for a plot of land, 6 per cent for a private purchase.

Gestor, Abogado and Notary

The first two are obvious. The notary will charge a registration fee, and occasionally for his services (the vendor usually pays for these). The registration fee is calculated from the registered value of the property.

Rates

There are two sorts of rates payable: the town and country rates, and rates charged by local authorities for such services as sewerage. They are usually paid once a year between 15 September and 15 November but sometimes twice a year – depending on the area. Notification of payment due is not usually given and fines of 20 per cent of the amount due will be imposed if the rates are not paid on time. Thus if you are going to be away it may be worth getting a friend, or paying an agency, to take care of bills. If the bills are not paid, the town hall (*Ayuntamiento*) can register a charge against the property and even place an 'embargo' on it. Cases have occured when a property has been lost due to lack of payment.

In some areas surcharges on the rates are imposed. Although these have been declared illegal, the authorities have no policy for automatic refunds and it is up to the individual to reclaim the money.

Utilities

The Spanish are very strict in this area. You will receive bills every two months for electricity and water. If these are not paid promptly you will be cut off. The same applies to gas supplies. Re-connection can be costly.

TROUBLESHOOTING

In the past, newcomers to Spain have been curiously trusting and indiscriminating when buying property. Whether due to a surfeit of sun or travel brochures, it has certainly cost a great many people a great deal of money. In fact you should exercise about ten times the normal amount of caution when buying anything, let alone property, in Spain.

This statement is borne out by the frequent publicity given to property scandals. These outrages are frequently perpetrated by foreigners on other foreigners. Edward McMillan-Scott, MEP, puts the number of Britons who have bought holiday homes at more than half a million. He has mail sacks filled with their complaints about every type of default in services not provided, incorrect descriptions, lack of planning permission, no basic services and so on.

International publicity given to the many existing property rackets fails to effect any sort of control although the EU has begun to investigate. It may be of some comfort that even Spaniards get caught too. Two of the latest cases concern some fifty retired Spanish couples in San Sebastián who paid deposits of hundreds of millions of pesetas to a property developer who then left the country, and a flat in Torremolinos which was sold 23 times to different buyers.

If you would like to contact Edward McMillan-Scott you will find his address at the back of this book.

Another company designed to prevent people from becoming victims was formed by the Norwegian, Per Svensson, at the start of the 1980s. It is called the *Instituto de Propietarios Extranjeros* (Institute of Foreign Property Owners) and the address is at the back of the book. It was originally formed to review all the pitfalls involved in buying Spanish property.

Yet another organisation with the same aim is the Foreign Advice Bureau (FAB) in Torremolinos. It is manned by voluntary polyglot staff. As Señorita Rosa de la Prada, whose family founded the Bureau, comments, 'In Spain, 85 per cent of offices, both official and private, speak only Spanish. So that immediately poses problems to many foreigners who do not master our language.' She herself speaks six languages and offers advice on a variety of subjects. Needless to say, this organisation is kept very busy so if you want to call in their offices, you should make an appointment. Again, you will find the address at the back of the book.

5

Driving in Spain

ACQUIRING A VEHICLE

If you choose to run a British registered car in Spain you must remember to keep it legally roadworthy in the United Kingdom. Otherwise the Spanish insurance will become invalid and the car will be illegal in Spain. This means that you must keep ready the car's latest MOT certificate and make sure that the UK road tax licence is displayed in the car.

Using your existing car

If you do not intend to stay in Spain for longer than six months at any one time, all you need is insurance. The insurance coverage available under EU regulations is basic. If you want anything extra you will have to arrange it with your insurance company (and pay for it).

The main drawback to this scheme is that the car will be seized by Customs if you go over the six-month limit and you may be unable to recover it.

On the other hand you could keep your car and change the number plates for Spanish ones. You would then be able to use the car while you are in Spain, but if you leave, the car can be sealed by Customs.

Making a tax-free export

You may choose to buy a new car in the United Kingdom (foreign or British make) and export it to Spain to avoid paying VAT in the United Kingdom. To do this you would have to buy the car direct from the manufacturer or sole agent and fill in Form VAT 411. The vendor will supply you with the form. You must then meet the following conditions:

- The car must be taken to Spain during the course of the next six months although you may use it in the United Kingdom during this time.

- Once you have taken the car abroad, it must stay there for a minimum of twelve months although you may bring it back for short periods.

- During this twelve-month period the car is for your sole use.

If you do not comply with these conditions, even if someone steals your car and takes it to the United Kingdom, the Customs and Excise will seize your car and you will never be able to get it back. For this reason it may be wise, in that first year abroad, to insure the car to its tax-free value plus the amount of VAT payable.

However, if you manage to get through all this without mishap, you may take your car home and sell it without incurring VAT at the end of the twelve months.

Importing your car

This can be an *extremely* time-consuming activity added to which it is almost impossible to determine how much must be paid in Customs and Excise duty and other taxes. It can be done if you have patience or a good *gestor*. There used to be a convenient Customs loophole whereby you could deliberately allow your car to go over the legal time limit. The foreign owner would be fined and the vehicle seized and auctioned. The proceeds of the auction less the small fine would be given to the owner who had, of course, bought his car back. However, even in those days it depended on the goodwill of the local Customs officer. In my case his wife was English.

If you do decide to import your car legally you will find leaflet V526 helpful. It can be obtained from your local Vehicle Licensing Office. You should complete Section 2 on the back of your Vehicle Registration Document and return it to the Vehicle Licensing Office who will provide you in return with a Certificate of Export, V561.

It is possible to avoid paying excise duty on your car if you have owned it for less than six months before you plan to leave for Spain. In that case you must sign a declaration at the Spanish Consulate in Britain or British Consulate in Spain that you are never going to return to the United Kingdom. You must also have proof that you have paid VAT on the car. The car will then be re-registered in Spain. You may not sell or transfer the car for twelve months afterwards.

Buying a Spanish car
This could save many of the headaches incurred by all the en-
counters with officialdom if you try to import a car.

Back in the 1960s, almost the only cars to be seen on Spanish
roads were products of the SEAT factory in Barcelona, Fiat
models 600 and 1500. Nowadays every type of car is seen. Many
are produced in the huge auto plants in Aragón, Galicia, Valencia,
Madrid, Barcelona, Pamplona and elsewhere. The multinationals
export these cars to many countries. If you were to visit one of
these auto plants you would see foreign quality control tech-
nicians conducting the final checks as rigorously as in their home
country.

As there is no restriction on make of car these days you can
choose from a huge selection. However, if you do buy a new car,
you will be liable to IVA (the Spanish equivalent of VAT) at the
rate of 16 per cent. A used car attracts 4 per cent IVA.

If you want to avoid paying IVA, you may consider buying a
tax-free car with tourist plates. During the first six months, special
dealers will be only too pleased to do all the paperwork to provide
you with a tax-free car. It does not have to be new. However,
you must pay in foreign currency and the normal hire purchase
arrangements do not apply. You may get permission to run the car
extended up to five years. Most companies which offer tax-free
cars guarantee re-purchase, so if you are not likely to be staying
in Spain for as long as five years, it is well worth considering
this solution to the motoring problem. The paperwork may be
handled at a *gestoría*. You will see many cars with special tourist
plates.

There are disadvantages to this system, however. Tourist plates
have to be renewed every six months and you will have to visit the
Jefatura de Tráfico (the local government-run car administration
service). It costs about 10,000 pesetas a year to use tourist plates
and if you wish to leave the country for longer than two months
you will have to get the plates sealed. When you return you will
have to visit the Customs and the *Guardia Civil* to get the plates
unsealed.

SPANISH REGISTERED NUMBER PLATES

The first letter denotes the province, or if two letters, the provincial capital. This is to distinguish the provinces whose names

begin with the same letter. Then there are four numbers and two letters (issued independently in each province) to indicate the age of the car. Thus the latest registrations in Madrid are in the range: (first EEC blue flash) M1234BB. You will find that most vehicles seem to remain in the province of their origin except in holiday periods. Naturally trucks are an exception.

If you would like to identify the cars you see on the roads the list in Figure 7 will be useful. It could also provide the basis for a game to amuse small children on a long journey.

There are 58 different vehicle registration letters in this list but there are only 50 Spanish provinces. The other eight include one each for the two North African enclaves of Spain (Ceuta and Melilla) and the rest are State related: *Ejército de Tierra* (ET), the Army, *Fuerzas Aereas* (EA), the Air Force, *Fuerzas Navales* (FN), the Navy, *Ministerio de Obras Publicas* (MOP), Ministry of Public Works, *Parque Guardia Civil* (PGC), to look out for, *Parque Movile Ministerios* (PMM), Civil Service vehicles in general.

If you buy a used car in Spain you should pay some attention to the registration plates and buy a car which has the same plates as that of the province where you are planning to live. If you do not, and buy, say, a car with a Zaragoza number plate and you live in or near Málaga, you will soon be known as 'the person from Zaragoza' even though you may be German, Norwegian or British. This may be annoying but is nothing compared to a car with a Vizcaya registration. Since the Vizcaya region is subject to a lot of terrorist activity, such cars are very unpopular in the rest of Spain, and are more likely to be detained by the *Guardia Civil*. If you think you are on to an unusually good bargain with a used car, perhaps you should check that the number plate is not prefixed with BI.

DRIVING LICENCE REQUIREMENTS

The pink and green UK driving licence issued by the DVLA since 1990 is acceptable in all EU countries, and has been valid for all purposes in Spain since 1 July 1996. Thus British residents in Spain no longer have to exchange their British driving licence for a Spanish one. They can therefore drive with a normal EU licence.

The green-coloured British driving licence is only accepted if used by tourists and accompanied by an official translation into Spanish (which we understand is available from the Spanish Embassy in London). Holders of these licences may prefer to use an International Driving Licence issued anywhere outside Spain.

Matriculas Nacionales

Province etc	Letters	Province etc	Letters
Álava	VI	Lérida	L
Albacete	AB	Logroño	LO
Alicante	A	Lugo	LU
Almería	AL	Madrid	M
Ávila	AV	Málaga	MA
Badajoz	BA	Melilla	ML
Balaeres	PM	Minis. Obras. Pub	MOP
Barcelona	BA	Murcia	MU
Burgos	BU	Navarra	NA
Cáceres	CC	Orense	OR
Cádiz	CA	Oviedo	O
Castellón	CS	Palencia	P
Ceuta	CE	Parque Guardia Civil	PGC
Ciudad Real	CR	Parque Mov. Min.	PMM
Córdoba	CO	Pontevedra	PO
Coruña	C	Salamanca	SA
Cuenca	CU	Santander	S
Ejército de Tierra	ET	Segovia	SG
Ejéricto de Aire	EA	Sevilla	SE
Fuerzas Navales	FN	Soria	SO
Gerona	GE	Tarragona	T
Granada	GR	Tenerife	TF
Gran Canaria	GC	Teruel	TE
Guadalajara	GU	Toledo	TO
Guipúzcoa	SS	Valencia	V
Huelva	H	Valladolid	VA
Huesca	HU	Vizcaya	BI
Jaén	J	Zamora	ZA
León	LE	Zaragoza	Z

Fig. 7. Spanish number plates

Medical certificates

At one time the medical certificate would be issued by the family doctor who performed some elementary tests. Now the tests have been brought up to EU standards and are carried out in special clinics.

These clinics are easy to find in towns and cities. They are usually clearly labelled, either *Centro de Reconocimento Médico para toda Clase de Permisos de Conducir* or *Centro de Reconocimientos Conductores y Armas todas las Categorias* (because hunters also have to be tested before they may obtain firearm licences and other documentation). They are open from 10.00 until 14.00 and 16.00 and 20.00 on weekdays and provide other treatments such as physiotherapy and saunas. Personnel in these clinics are normally friendly and co-operative.

The clinics are equipped with a full range of medical and electronic equipment to test your senses and reflexes and you cannot cheat. The medical normally takes half an hour and costs 2,700 pesetas if you are under 70. When you reach this venerable age and have to pass yearly medicals, they are free.

Once you have obtained your certificate of physical fitness you should have no difficulty in obtaining your pink Spanish *Permiso de Conducción* (driving licence).

Types of driving licence

Different types of licences are issued for different types of vehicle and are subject to different regulations. A B1 licence is issued to drivers of cars and vans up to 3.5 tonnes. An A1 or A2 licence is issued to motorbike riders and must be renewed every three years. A C licence is issued to truck drivers. A D licence is issued to bus drivers and an E licence to drivers of heavy vehicles with trailers.

You must carry your driving licence at all times whenever or wherever you drive on the public highways, even when clad in shorts. If you fail to do so a strict policeman may fine you – and not even a bikini will help! Nor talking in English, German etc.

If you lose your licence or it is stolen (and this happens to many foreigners) it is very easy to replace and will only take about half an hour in an off-peak period. You should go to the local *Jefatura de Tráfico*. The *Jefatura de Tráfico* handles all matters related to road transport, driving, car usage and ownership. It is usually filled with fast-moving queues and there are 'No Smoking' signs which are fairly effective.

UNDERSTANDING LEGAL REQUIREMENTS FOR DRIVERS

Spanish legislation is strict about the equipment and documentation that should be carried when you are driving. These are the items you must have before you make any trip:

- A complete set of spare light bulbs and tools for changing them if a bulb fails.

- The spare wheel which should have the same pressure as the other four, and the tools necessary for changing a wheel.

- Two warning triangles. If you have an enforced stop due to a puncture, repairs etc they must be displayed and clearly visible about 50 metres fore and aft of your vehicle.

- All the documents relating to car ownership. If you take your car to a garage to be serviced you may also be asked for these.

- Up-to-date insurance coverage. A receipt must be kept in your car – the police can issue a fine if this is not available.

- Your driving licence.

You must have all of these when you travel. If the police should ever stop you, they will check every single item on this list.

ITV (Inspección Técnico de Vehiculos)
Any Spanish vehicle over five years old must pass the equivalent of the British MOT every year. The test is called the ITV and costs about 5,000 pesetas. Official ITV centres are easily visible throughout Spain.

After the car has been tested you will receive a blue form listing all the possible faults. If the car has failed, the relevant sections of the blue form will be underlined and you have fifteen days to repair the car. If you can, you should get the examiner to write down for you exactly what needs to be done so that you can show it to the garage who will be repairing the vehicle. If you do not do this the garage may get over-enthusiastic and present you with an enormous bill for repairs.

Transferencia (transfer document)
If you buy a used Spanish car you should insist on receiving a *transferencia* from the vendor. The vendor should fill it in and

the document will transfer ownership to you. The form itself is available from the *Jefatura de Tráfico*. This will also free you from paying any fines not paid by the previous owner – which could be very expensive!

Municipal road tax

This ranges from 5,400 pesetas for cars under 12 hp to over 14,000 pesetas for cars with higher power ratings. It is normally paid between March and April and the *Ayuntamiento* should send you a reminder. However, if it gets lost in the post as 111,758 items did in 1989 according to the *Dirección General de Correos*, you should pay regardless. If you do not, you will have to pay a 20 per cent surcharge on the bill. The tax itself is called the *Impuesto Municipal sobre la Circulación de Vehiculos* and may be paid at the Council's tax collection office (*oficina municipal de impuestos*) if you can face an hour long wait in the queue. Otherwise you may send a postal order (*giro postal*), or bank order, or get the *gestoría* to deal with the matter. Payment via a bank is the simplest.

The tax must be paid by all vehicles registered and used in Spain so it is very fair and compared with the car licence fee in other countries it is quite cheap.

Taxation is on the 'up and up' in Spain in all areas, and vehicles suffer as much as any so it is best to check.

Nowadays you can pay through a bank which is much simpler and cuts waiting time.

Seat belts

Spanish legislation requires seatbelts to be worn. When you drive out from a city, town or village you will see a large blue notice reminding you to buckle up. If you ignore it, you may be fined and as Spanish car insurance agents say that the average accident rate is two or three times higher in Spain than in France, it could also be a wise precaution. Every long weekend brings a death toll of between 50 and 100 on Spanish highways.

Don't drink and drive

All Stevie Wonder's exhortations on the subject are borne out by Spanish legislation. Breath tests may be carried out even when you have been driving perfectly correctly and there are heavy penalties for those who exceed the limit, which is *very* strict.

Normally two small beers or one cognac or whisky is *all* that is permitted.

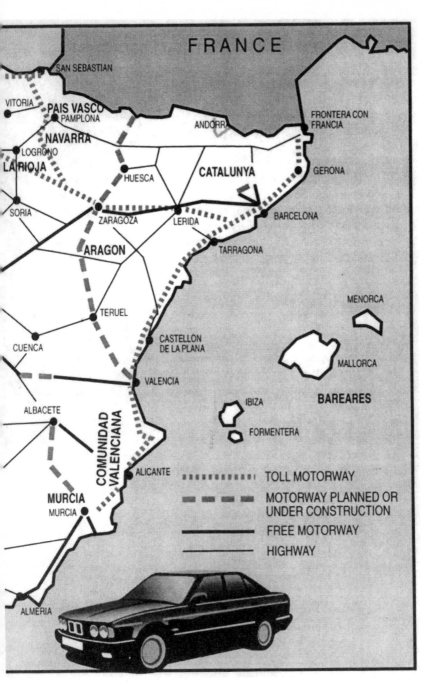

Fig. 8. The Spanish motorway system.

Lights

Obviously lights should be turned on at dusk or before, as you do not always notice the fading light. There are other circumstances, however, when lights should be used and these are worth mentioning:

- when it is raining or snowing

- when you travel through a tunnel

- in underground car parks.

If you do not use lights in these circumstances you can be fined. You should not use lights when you park by the roadside at night.

USING MOTORWAY ROUTES

The main motorway routes which are toll roads go down the Mediterranean seaboard to Alicante. There is little delay in negotiating Valencia (which used to be such a bottle-neck). The motorways are being extended to Murcia and Cartagena and are planned to link up with Gibraltar, and eventually, maybe, even Africa, by spanning the Straits of Gibraltar with a wonderbridge or by tunnelling underneath.

The other main motorways are from Panadés, between Barcelona and Tarragona, and go north and west to Pamplona, Bilbao and Burgos with an extension to Santander. Other isolated stretches exist in various parts of the country, see Figure 8, pages 80–81.

The A-6 starts north-west of Madrid and runs for 108 kms to Adanero on the La Coruña highway.

The A-4 links Seville with Cádiz running for 113 kms through flat country.

The A-66 avoids the Pass of Pajares, starting near León and ending after 77.5 kms near Oviedo in the foothills of the Cantábrica mountains.

The A-9, 74 kms long, links La Coruña with Santiago de Compostela. After that there are 57 kms of crowded main roads as far as Pontevedra and 28 kms of motorway to Vigo. Work on bridging the gap between Santiago and Pontevedra has stopped. It will be a long time before this section is completed since the topography is so difficult.

The Government is investing large amounts into its road construction plans in an effort to improve Spanish driving. *Autovías* (bypasses) are being constructed on all the radial routes from Madrid, the one from Madrid to Zaragoza being particularly welcome. These roads are toll-free and quite fast.

Much caution should be exercised, even on some main roads. Standards leave much to be desired. Foreign truck drivers show little of the courtesy of drivers of Spanish trucks, and care is needed.

DRIVING HAZARDS

Speed limits

So you have crossed the border with your car. Did you notice the speed limits? Normally, they are displayed clearly at every vehicle entry point into Spanish territory. The theory is as follows:

	kmph	mph
motorways which are toll roads (*autopistas*)	120	75
Autopistas with four or more lanes or three lane main roads and highways	100	62.5
Other main roads and inter-town connections	90	56.2
In population centres and where indicated	60	37.5

The practice is very different. Many Spanish drivers travel at speeds well over the legal limit. Many modern cars travel the *autopistas* and *autovías* at 150–200 kmph, while a few try to beat their personal best from A to B. Although the maximum speeding fine is 50,000 pesetas with confiscation of licence in bad cases, it does not seem much of a deterrent.

You may notice traffic lights in some towns and villages, especially in the north and west. If you are travelling at more than 50/60 kmph they will turn red automatically and are an effective means of enforcing speed limits. Shooting the lights, especially in the cities, carries a heavier fine.

If you are caught you will be fined on the spot. If you choose to pay on the spot you will be allowed a 20 per cent reduction. If you do not, the fine will be sent to your home, by registered post, even as far as Scotland or Finland.

Beware if you spot a car by the roadside with PGC (*Parque Guardia Civil*) numberplates. It could be photographing speeding vehicles. The photograph is considered to be sufficient proof of speeding and you will be fined. Another more recent tactic is for one PGC car to be stationed at the start of a town or village and another to be stationed a mile or more down the road. The first car will radio details of offenders to the second car which will then stop the guilty parties. Unmarked police cars are also being used these days to take photographs.

You should also be warned that it no longer works to pretend to be an uncomprehending Englishman. These days it is 'pay up or else' and you will be handed a polyglot instruction sheet to help you understand.

Roadworks

These present one of the greatest driving dangers in Spain. One minute you may be bowling blissfully along a brand new *autovía* and the next, facing a bewildering array of multi-coloured traffic signs and lines on the road surface going all over the place. If you should be unfortunate enough to be experiencing heavy rain and on-coming traffic, it might just be better to make an overnight stop and start again in the morning when visibility will be better.

When you see the road works signs you should reduce speed and take it very easy. Then you should follow the yellow or orange lines painted on the road as they take priority over the normal white ones. Sometimes there will be several sets of lines in different colours and you will be very confused. That is why you should drive carefully to avoid accidents.

Short cuts and delays

Map readers should be very wary of short cuts. Once off the main roads in Spain, you will find the standard falls to third world levels. Although you may save many kilometres in distance the trips will take hours longer and you may be exhausted afterwards.

For example, if you are driving from Garrucha or Mojácar in Almería to Granada and you are in a hurry, you should ignore the apparent short cut through Gérgal on the C-325. It took me an hour's rally driving to cover 33 kms on something that was little more than a mountain track. There was no traffic, just a continuous succession of tight curves. It would have been much quicker to stick to the main N-340 and N-324. Similarly from Jerez de la Frontera to Gibraltar. You should stick to the main N-340 again. It is quicker to travel from Madrid to Pamplona via Zaragoza than to try the shorter distance via Soria. The same applies from Lérida to Andorra. The parallel routes are definitely to be avoided.

It really depends whether you are prepared to sacrifice a good deal of time. The off-beat routes can be very attractive but the slow average speed in the mountainous zones of the southern Pyrenees, Santander, Asturias and Galicia has to be experienced to be believed. When time is of the essence the expense of the motorways becomes worthwhile. Other notoriously slow routes are the approach roads to Cuenca, and from Vínaroz (Castellón) to the mediaeval city of Morella.

Traffic signs

The most perilous of these is the triangular sign 'Give way to on-coming traffic', usually found at T junctions. Sometimes, however, it will be so placed that on-coming traffic may cut clean across your bows, the idea being that when one traffic flow has greater priority than another, the first may cross the road directly in front of the second. So if you see a large triangular sign at the roadside and another triangle painted on the road, watch out.

Flashing amber lights may mean that you are approaching roadworks, or that traffic lights are not working or even a police roadblock (often seen after a terrorist killing, or some other hazard). But the most dangerous signal of all is the green 'walk' signal at the end of the pedestrian phase of the traffic lights, because, unknown to the British pedestrian, the drivers will be seeing a flashing amber light. Equally the unwary British driver will not be expecting pedestrians to cross as a matter of right. So special caution should be exercised around these lights.

Accidents

If you are unlucky enough to be involved in an accident, the *Guardia Civil* will soon arrive and take control. They are well used to dealing with drama and can be very helpful. They are usually very human people, anxious to help and very well trained and equipped to do so. If a vehicle bearing the sign '*Atestado*' appears it means that the people in it are there to bear witness. The best attitude to adopt with all traffic policemen is that of complete co-operation. Belligerent comments may literally cost you dear.

GREATEST DANGER

The greatest danger of all for the British is crossing the road. The author has saved many Brits from being run down that were looking in the wrong direction when crossing the road. If you have never or hardly ever travelled outside the United Kingdom, you will be unaccustomed to looking left first before you cross the road.

Equally, once you have become accustomed to living in Spain, you will have to adapt to looking right before you cross the road. Care is also needed on your trips back to the United Kingdom.

GUARDING AGAINST CAR THEFTS AND ROBBERY

Another source of annoyance to the car owner is the frequency of car theft. Many people leave their cars in the street overnight. In that case you should fit alarms, have your car windows engraved with the car's registration number, fit a steering lock and generally take as many precautions as you can. Perhaps the best tip when you are travelling is to leave the car in an overnight car park. Failing that you should park it under a working street lamp in a good neighbourhood.

Car radios disappear with great frequency in this country. Removable radios are very popular. You will often see a group of friends in a bar, each with his car radio to hand. The modern locking radios may be useful or you could simply try to cover your radio in some way.

The usual method of stealing from cars is to use a number of steel balls on a chain to break a window. The radio will be seized and anything else of value that is in full view and then the thief will beat a hurried retreat. The long queues in the police stations (*comisarios*) to report stolen property bear witness to the size of the problem.

The latest most vexing habit is the custom of removing car insignia which fetch black market prices for use as keyrings.

USEFUL TIPS

Petrol stations
When Spain entered the European Community in 1986, petrol
stations should in theory have sprung up all over the country.
However, the Administration delayed progress in every way
possible. Finally in the 1990s, opposition was overcome and the
national total began to rise:

1990	5,391
1995	6,390
1997	6,875
1998	7,093 (planned)
1999	7,335 (planned)
2000	7,600 (planned)

Now new petrol stations belonging to BP, ELF, Total, Petrogal,
etc. are to be seen everywhere.

It is still a wise precuation to keep the tank topped up, especially if you are going off the beaten track. Another time to take
special care is in winter when there are snowfalls. The car heater
could stop you from freezing to death if you are caught in a
snowdrift.

Some petrol stations give better measures than others. Campsa
and Shell have a good reputation, especially the self-service
pumps. When you settle in Spain, you should conduct a personal
market survey before deciding on 'your' filling station.

Garages
As has been mentioned, you cannot always trust these to carry out
the work you would like. It is a good idea to take along a Spanish
speaking companion. If, however, you are not satisfied with a
particular garage, shop around until you find one you can trust or
someone recommends one. Eventually, when you have been a
Spanish resident for a while, the newness will wear off and you
will be treated more like a local.

Warning lights
Warning lights are used a great deal in Spain, especially on the
autovias and *autopistas* when an emergency halt may be very
dangerous with so many speeding drivers about.

It is worth remembering that if the *Guardia Civil* feel mean you may be fined for neglecting to indicate after overtaking to bear right as well as before this manoeuvre.

Bicycles
Spanish roads are definitely not for bicycles. Hundreds of cyclists die every year on roads with just enough room for two cars to pass each other but no room for a cyclist. A few cyclist-only tracks are being laid alongside modern roads but there is a long way to go to reach EU standards for cyclists.

If you see that a cycle race is planned, you should try to get away from the route as soon as possible. Bicycles have right of way and you may have to drive behind them for a long distance.

Roundabouts
These have the same legislation as in the United Kingdom, but often Spaniards do not obey the give-way rule, especially drivers from more remote provinces, such as Zamora.

Spanish drivers
These are not noted for their patience so try not to slow down too much when rounding corners, and do not hesitate at the traffic lights. Some drivers are prone to hit the indicators while talking so be wary.

Some good points about Spanish driving
One welcome change is to find that Spanish truck drivers are some of the most considerate in the world. They will help you to overtake by warning you when there is an on-coming vehicle and they generally set a good example for their counterparts in other nations. They have a co-operative attitude that lightens the driving load on long trips.

Traffic signs are good in Spain although at times there may seem to be too many of them, but they help to make for road safety. In Huelva, Zamora, Lugo, Asturias and Almería they may not be as good, as fanatics for the regional languages will deface them.

The traffic police (*Guardia Civil de Tráfico*) too are good. They may turn up if you break down and give you the benefit of their mechanical knowledge. They are also skilled in first aid as they are often first at the scene of an accident. In some areas, they can summon a helicopter to fly accident victims to hospital – a major time-saving where there are secondary roads.

6

Staying Healthy

ADOPTING A HEALTHIER WAY OF LIFE

One of the best ways of improving your health is to adopt the Spanish way of life when you go to live in Spain. While many in the United States are going crazy over the 'new' Mediterranean diet the Spanish have been following it for centuries; cooking with olive oil, eating plenty of fruit and vegetables of all types, having wine with the midday meal and taking a *siesta*. Doctors now think all these increase your life expectancy. Even though the successful business person may not have time for a *siesta*, for those who do, like retired people and the self-employed, it means that you can start the day anew every twelve hours.

If you share the Spanish way of life and eat with a Spanish family you will notice that fish and seafood of all kinds are frequently eaten in a huge variety of dishes. In fact, while the EU average for fish consumption is about 14 kgs a year per capita, in Spain it is closer to 30 kgs and used to be even higher. Doctors announce more and more of their discoveries which prove that fish, fish oils and other fishy elements can help you to a longer life.

The popularity of fish and seafood in Spain is borne out by visiting the numerous markets (*mercados*) to be found in all towns, large or small. You will find many fresh fish stalls. Hake is the most common type of fish, but nowadays you will find an increasing variety of other species, including salmon from Scandinavia and even Scotland at times. In the United Kingdom it is becoming increasingly difficult to find a fresh fish shop, but in Spain they are everywhere. There are also a great many frozen food stalls where seafood is sold in bulk. There should be no difficulty in producing attractive fish dishes as so many Spanish cookery books are being published.

Bizcocho de Zanahorias
2 tazas de harina
2 cucharaditas de levadura
½ cucharadita de bicarbonato
2 cucharaditas de canela
1 cucharadita de sal

4 huevos
2 tazas de azúcar
1 taza de aceite vegetal (lo más suave posible)

3 tazas de zanahoria picada (muy pequeño)
½ taza de nueces picadas (muy pequeño)

Mezclar los ingredientes secos juntos; (en otro cacerola) mezclar el azucar, aceite y huevos (uno por uno); añadir los ingredientes secos poco a poco hasta que esté todo junto, entonces añadir las zanahorias y las nueces.

Meter al horneo en un molde engrasado y enharinado unos 45 minutos, a una temperatura de 350° ó 400°.

Carrot Cake
2 cups of flour
2 teaspoons of baking powder
Half teaspoon of bicarbonate of soda
2 teaspoons of cinnamon
1 teaspoon of salt

4 eggs
2 cups of sugar
1 cup of olive oil (low acidity)

3 cups of finely grated carrot
Half cup of walnuts, broken up fine

Mix all the dry ingredients together; in one saucepan, add the sugar and the oil. Add eggs one by one. Add the dry ingredients and lastly the carrots and nuts. Mix well.

Place in a greased, floured tin, and bake for about 45 minutes at 350°–400° F, 200° C, Gas Mark 4–5.

Fig. 9. A typical Spanish recipe. The word recipe from the Latin *recipere* meaning to take.

Given the huge variety in Spanish cuisine and the house-proud nature of many Spanish *amas de casa* (mistresses or literally bosses of the house) it is claimed that a different dish could be served at every meal for a whole year. This is feasible – but it might be expensive.

Many of the older housewives are glad to pass on their private recipes. These are often much better than those in the expensive cookery books. In exchange they could be interested in shepherd's pie, steak and kidney pie or other European recipes.

Thus you may receive a recipe from your neighbour like that in Figure 9, 'from Ana to Margarita, hoping it turns out well'. It turned out to be carrot cake – and very tasty too. If you find the translation of your recipe difficult you will probably find a friendly person to show you exactly what to do.

As well as swapping recipes and mixing with people, the *siesta* is important. It is described by Dr A. Culebras-Fernández as particularly beneficial to older people and working people, there being no harm in taking your daily quota of sleep in two doses instead of the northern European habit of just one. The sleeping requirements of an adult vary between from five and nine hours per day, so it is obvious that the Spanish need their *siesta* since they go to bed well after midnight and leave for work at 07.00 in the morning, bright and cheerful. Dr Culebras recommends an hour's *siesta* for people past forty. Churchill circumscribed his *siesta* to twenty minutes after acquiring the habit when he was a war correspondent in Cuba in 1898.

A relaxed attitude to life

This is most noticeable in southern Spain and weakens as you go northwards. Statistics show that cardiovascular deaths dropped in the 1980s in Spain and life expectancy increased from 72.3 years of age in 1970 to 76.4 years in 1985. This is above the European average of 74.4 and ahead of the United Kingdom, France and Germany. Infant mortality in the rest of Europe is lower only in Finland, Sweden and Switzerland. And as usual the ladies outlive the gentlemen.

EXPLORING PREVENTIVE MEDICINE

Spas (*balnearios*) are a very popular form of preventive medicine. They are often set in the most beautiful scenery like La Toja on a pine-covered island off the coast of Galicia, Panticosa in the Pyrenees, San Juan de la Fontsanta in Majorca, Lanjarón, 50 kms from Málaga and so on. They treat rheumatism, all types of digestive disorders and many other ailments, while helping to raise health standards and providing a leisure break from the stress and strain of modern business. The *balneario* habit is growing in Spain again after some years of decline, when it was considered old-fashioned. Now it has become very fashionable and many of them are being modernised.

The general set up for these *balnearios* is to have a main hotel with thermal baths and treatments from a hot spring with waters of medicinal properties. A full medical staff provides the treatment which may cost between a quarter and a half of a million pesetas for a ten-day stay. However, there are usually cheaper hotels, *pensions* or lodgings nearby, so that treatment costs need not be as expensive. Many Spaniards are enthusiasts and go year after year convinced that their health is improved. The *balnearios* are also patronised by the French and some other nationalities.

There are about 100 of these establishments in Spanish territory ranging from a humble one or two star hostel to the five star luxury hotel of La Toja which was founded in the last century and is still the venue for many Spanish VIPs during the summer recess. They follow in the steps of the Romans who were some of the first to discover their benefits. An excellent map, *Mapa de Estaciones Termales, Balnearios*, is publishd by the *Secretaría General de Turismo*. If your local tourist office does not have a copy you could try writing to the head office in Madrid.

The map lists 59 *balnearios* showing their location and giving approximate distances from the nearest main towns. The full address of each is given, period when open (normally from June to September), the composition of the spring waters, treatments given, altitude, number of rooms and so on. They have five main regional associations who are glad to deal with queries and a national association ANET. The addresses are:

Asociación Nacional de Estaciones Termales (ANET), calle Martín de los Heros, 23-4° dcha B, 28008 Madrid. Tel: 91 542 97 75. Fax: 91 542 98 24.

Asociación Catalana de la Propiedad Balnearia, Paseo de Gracia 34-1°, 08007 Barcelona. Tel: 93 317 03 12. Fax: 93 865 23 12.

Asociación Gallega de la Propiedad Balnearia, Hotel La Toja, 36991 Isla de la Toja, El Grove (Pontevedra). Tel: 986 73 00 25. Fax: 986 73 12 01.

Asociación Balnearia, calle Balmes 191-5°-4/B, 08006 Barcelona. Tel: 93 218 36 00. Fax: 93 217 10 95.

Asociación Valenciana de Estaciones Termales, calle Jesús 44-2° – 3ª 46007 Valencia. Tel: 96 325 99 01.

Just within the Iberian Peninsula in the pocket principality of Andorra is the five star Hotel Roc Blanc which merits a special mention in the field of medicine. Skilled medical staff provide a complete geriatric programme using hot spring water and all the modern treatments to ensure that older folk feel youthful. This medical programme of rejuvenation is undertaken by doctors and fully qualified medical staff with many years of experience.

The Hotel Roc Blanc gives excellent service. It is located in the centre of Andorra, surrounded by first class shops, and has the attraction of tax-free shopping, even though surrounded by other territories. The 'cuisine' of the hotel is also fully recommended. It is better than many modern hotels there, as it has considerable history, having welcomed people fleeing for their lives, under the Franco regime, and helping them as refugees.

Also the important spa treatment centre of Les Escaldes is fully functional, again with every type of spa treatment, as well as being a recreation centre with every type of application. Even if expensive, it is often crowded, as its luxury standard attracts many regulars. Address:

Plaza Coprinceps, 5 Andorra. Tel: 376 82 14 86. Fax: 376 86 02 44. Telex: 224.

USING NATURAL MEDICINES

The age-old herbal treatments and other natural medicines have become very popular in Spain during the last decade. Many of these treatments have the great advantage of no bad side-effects. In most towns and cities nowadays it is easy to find shops which supply products by Dr Vogel of Switzerland, whose books and natural medicines are known world-wide. Other Spanish concerns also supply special dietary foods and treatments. One of these is Prodiet which manufactures 300 products and claims that sales in 1989 increased by 30 per cent to reach 900 million pesetas. The main factory is in Igualada (Barcelona) with smaller ones in Vitoria (Álava) and Pinto (Madrid) and there is a nationwide distribution system.

If you would like to contact a naturalist doctor or herbalist you should ask in one of the shops. Some have consulting rooms, others will have contacts.

Treatments can be expensive but effective. As always it is wise to be cautious and ask the locals. There are quacks and fanatics in Spain, just as anywhere else, and they can be *very* expensive.

The best doctors are those who have studied traditional medicine and branched out into this new/ancient art. They can inform you from both sides of medicine that pumpkin seeds may help cure prostate problems, porridge may help improve eyesight, that an instant cure for a persistent cough is to place a cold damp cloth on the nape of the neck, etc., etc.

If you are interested in other forms of natural medicine these may also be found. Foreign doctors, dentists and other professions are now permitted to practise in Spain under EU regulations and they sometimes advertise in the many foreign language publications in Spain. Again the herbalist shops can help with the addresses of local practitioners. But again beware of quacks and their expensive treatments.

UNDERSTANDING THE SPANISH HEALTH SERVICE

A brief outline

The Spanish national health service is known as the *Seguridad Social* or the *Insalud*. During recent years, this organisation, its services, and in general its manner of treating patients, have improved greatly. This has become especially notable since the PP Government came to power in May 1996. A visit to a doctor has become a pleasant experience with understanding personnel – in general – and good attention. Although there are waiting periods at times, one can make an appointment, which is often respected.

One reason for this change is that patients can now choose the doctor they prefer, which obviously places them in a stronger position than previously. Government instructions also percolate downwards and ensure 'better value for their money', so all in all, a welcome change has occurred. It should be noted, however, that some of the 17 regions now control their own health service, which can lead to differences. There may also be differences, because of particular personalities or for other reasons.

The general impression of improvement is based not only on personal experiences, but on facts and figures. The Presidente of *Insalud*, Alberto Núñez Feijoo, has given comparative figures for April 1996 and October 1997. During this period, waiting time for an operation has fallen from an average of 210 days to 115 days. The average stay in hospital has fallen from 9.14 to 8.37 days. Much of this advance has been made possible by treating people as out-patients, thus not requiring admission and a hospital bed. The number of operations per year has doubled from 25,203 to 50,762.

Señor Núñez says that because of this policy of keeping people out of hospital, they have saved 93,439 hospital/bed/days. 'This represents a saving equivalent to 2,570 more beds available, or five new hospitals with 500 beds each.' There are important plans for further improvements in service in 1998, including reducing the waiting period for operations to an average of 80 days. If the waiting period goes beyond that limit, then the patient should be able to go to a private hospital, with *Insalud* paying costs.

Emergency treatments

One method of gate-crashing is to go to the Emergency Admission Department, which is maintained, as you would expect, for victims of road accidents, heart attacks and similar urgent cases. In case you hesitate to do this a recent report from *Insalud* maintains that only a third of the patients who go to this department (*Urgencias*) genuinely require emergency treatment.

If you are treated by a doctor, you will receive first class treatment but there is every sign of the *Departmento de Urgencias* becoming snowed under with cases.

Services not supplied by *Insalud*

The *Seguridad Social* has always had the reputation for giving only basic coverage for medical and other needs, thus the only dental treatment available under its auspices is extraction of a rotten tooth. Glasses and other standard optical treatment are out, although cataract operations may be carried out if you meet the right doctor. Other subsidiary services are not provided either.

If you can, take advantage of all the medical services in your own country before you come to Spain. Visit your dentist, your optician, etc. Otherwise if you decide on private treatment you could copy many Spanish people and cross the border for better or cheaper treatment. This applies particularly in the north of Spain where many go to France for dental treatment, which is much cheaper there. In the south many cross the border to Gibraltar for the same reason.

Those eligible for *Insalud*
If you are living and working in Spain you will have to make social security payments. If a secretary earns about £200 per week receiving her wages monthly, she will have to pay 6 per cent of her earnings. She will be issued with a nine digit social security number which gives her the right to free basic medical treatment, reductions in the cost of medicines, also unemployment and sick pay. The *Gestor* can help self-employed persons or in difficult cases. Normally you will find that your employer will deal with the paperwork. People who do not work in Spain can opt to join the social security system. Pensioners may receive the benefits of Spanish social security even while receiving their pension payments directly from their home country.

If you are British you should write to the DSS for more information. According to the DSS there is no problem in receiving your United Kingdom pension payments while living in Spain, but in case you decide to return to the United Kingdom it is better to continue to have your pension paid by the British authorities. Since many of the foreign language publications in Spain carry advertisements for property in their home countries it suggests that many return. The DSS has a number of helpful leaflets for those who wish to reside abroad, which cover paying reduced Class II payments to permit a full pension entitlement and medical treatment on the British National Health Service if you should return to the United Kingdom. Other alternatives are available.

EXAMINING PRIVATE INSURANCE SCHEMES

There are a large number of private schemes available in Spain, but it is very important to read the small print on the policies of the Spanish ones. Some of these will only provide coverage in your home town or in a certain hospital and additional payments may have to be made for specialist and other treatments. When buying private medical insurance it is advisable to choose a policy offering repatriation in serious cases. Here is a description of some of the schemes available.

Sanitas
This used to be one of the most popular private insurance companies in Spain and it provides reasonable treatment. Many Spaniards use this after having had frightening experiences with *Insalud*. Just recently, however, this society has changed ownership, as a result of which the fees have increased. This has led to considerable protest, but it is still an attractive policy and may seem reasonably priced compared with those in other European countries.

The Westminster Private Medical Clinic
This clinic is in Gibraltar and is popular with many of the Costa del Sol residents. It offers a medical which may last between 45 minutes and three hours, working on the premise that prevention is better than cure. When a cure is necessary, all the specialists are available and most of their fees may be claimed on most private health insurance schemes. This clinic's motto is 'British Health Care For You and Your Family' and this can be reassuring in a strange land.

Danmark AS International Health Insurance
This company advertises in the foreign language publications and offers a very full range of services to a high standard. Danmark is well known on the Costa del Sol and recommended by many there as giving prompt payment for expenses incurred by all types of medical treatment including the most serious. Many people feel happier with a foreign-based company. This company has a representative office in Spain from which full details may be obtained.

BUPA International Lifeline
This company claims 'when it comes to overseas healthcare you'll find that BUPA goes to the ends of the earth to help'. It has special rates for people both below and over pensionable age. This company is recommended by many foreign residents and provides a complete service including repatriation if the case is serious enough. The initials stand for British United Provident Association.

Exeter Hospital Aid Society
This is another British company which aims to please and has a good reputation for its dealings with patients in Spain. Again it has a wide variety of policies available. Details of these may be obtained by writing to the UK address.

Other schemes
As there are so many foreign residents in Spain there are many Spanish schemes available. The locals will be able to tell you which are the best.

SPANISH HEALTH WARNING

One characteristic of medical services in Spain, especially those inland, is that August is a *deadly* month, *literally*. Statistics prove that many more die in this month than any other in the year. Why? The majority of doctors, specialists, etc. take a month's holiday during August leaving locums. Sometimes it is quite hard even to find a locum. So in all seriousness if you are smitten with a serious ailment in August you should consider seeking medical attention in another country. A book could be written on all the medical disasters known to have occurred in August in Spain.

7

Staying Wealthy

This chapter deals with the main everyday financial matters. A really complete guide to Spanish business and commercial matters would fill many volumes.

UNDERSTANDING THE BANKING SYSTEM

Banks figure high on the list of any visitors to Spain. Apart from the traditional Spanish banks, an increasing number of foreign ones are moving into Spain. Lloyds, Barclays and others are to be seen more and more often. The main national banks are the Hispano-Americano, the BBV (Banco Bilbao Vizcaya), Santander, the Popular, the Central, the Banco Español de Crédito, the Zaragozano and a large variety of savings banks united in one federation. All these offer normal banking services, but there are some differences. Whatever your plans, and however much you like Spain it is to be recommended that you do not close your UK bank account as the staff may be able to get results from your Spanish bank when you cannot.

Transfers

Spain and Portugal hold the record for the greatest delays in processing bank transfers in Europe. Thus, if you have to make a rapid transaction it may easily come unstuck even though you have the benefit of telex and other modern devices.

Once you have opened an account with a Spanish bank you can request your British bank to send the money direct but there may still be considerable delays. Somehow other banks will get involved and interfere. The best advice is to allow for delays when planning any transactions of this nature.

It is essential to have any transfer of capital or sums of importance fully documented. Nevertheless when the author was transferring capital from the United Kingdom to Spain to complete a property transaction, a large amount of money went 'missing.' The money reappeared only when threats were made to call in the police.

If you are a newcomer to Spain you may well try to pay in foreign cheques to your Spanish bank. You will be told that these have to be presented at a branch of a bank in the drawee's country. This may take a month or more so short cuts have to be found.

By the same token you may use these delays to your own advantage at times.

Normal Spanish bank usage

Any foreigner interested in opening a bank account in Spain is usually given a warm welcome and there are a wide range of services available. If you are acquiring a holiday home you can arrange for the bank to pay such accounts as the telephone, the electricity, the water, council rates and so on.

If you are a resident with plenty of time and a wish to keep an eye on the bills, you may pay the bills personally in cash into the appropriate utility's account at any bank branch. Personal attention may prevent you from paying the same bill twice like the time when *Telefónica* issued accounts twice for the same accounting period. The money was eventually refunded, but the amount of free credit must have run into many millions of pesetas.

However, since non-payment of bills may lead you into serious trouble it might be worth risking those standing orders, but checking the accounts carefully.

You will find that cheques are not used much in Spain. They are not accepted as a satisfactory method of payment by most hotels, garages, shops. Credit cards, however, are very popular and may be used for all sorts of shopping including the hypermarkets. Such cards as Visa, Access, Master Card, Eurocard and others are readily accepted against foreign accounts. This can be useful as your income may be paid into these and withdrawn as weekly shopping, petrol and other payments. Some supermarket chains produce their own credit cards, or rather security cards which means that they will accept a Spanish cheque, but only from known and trusted clients.

Some factors in your favour

These remarks apply to retired people, holiday-makers and the like, not business people.

Credit cards which enable cash to be withdrawn are used

universally in Spain. Cash dispensers may be found in most of the Spanish banks and they will accept foreign cards. In some towns, however, only one branch of a particular bank will accept them, in others every branch will. It is certainly a fact that these machines seem to function better if you request the Spanish instructions instead of the German, English, French or whatever other language may be offered. (The banks will deny this.)

Eurocheques

Eurocheques are a convenient method of paying for the weekly shopping, the petrol and other everyday items. They have the added advantage of taking a little time to be processed so that you may enjoy one or several weeks of credit. It is therefore worth finding out which bank takes the longest time to process Eurocheques. In general the savings banks (*cajas de ahorros*) are the quickest.

Purchases with the Visa card may also take a fairly long time in coming home to roost, another advantage in your favour. All documentation should be kept for five years. This is a legal requirement for Spanish taxation purposes.

Foreign banks

Entry into the European Union has meant that many restrictions on banking practices have been phased out. Ex-property owners no longer pack their suitcases full of bank-notes to take to Switzerland, or to send by courier to other countries. Restrictions do still apply to taking capital out of Spain so your bank should make proper records of your capital to permit you to release it to another country if you wish. Within the next year or two, the Spanish Administration will have no authority over your capital and the Common Market principles of free markets and free circulation of capital will be enforced, spelling the end of these unfair restrictions. In the meantime you should choose your bank carefully.

Credit Suisse could be the best bank for you with its excellent service and secrecy. Branches exist in most countries in the world (as well as in Madrid) and the most complicated instructions will be carried out reliably. Credit Suisse have an affiliated branch in Andorra called Credit Andorre. Again service is excellent and unlike most banks in other countries any request will be carried out on the date specified.

Offshore banking

Andorra is determined to become an offshore banking centre – 'but in its own particular manner, without copying any other centre, and seeing that it is an important part of our future,' the *Presidente* (CAP) of Andorra told me. All banks are represented in Andorra, local and foreign.

The Andorran banks have international recognition. Two are in the World Top 1000 Banks published by *The Banker*. In 771st place is Credit Andorre and in 986th place is the Banca International. They are founder members of the Andorran Banking Association which totals seven native banks, all anxious to help. The other banks are Cassany, Mora, Bacasa, La Caixa and the Banca Reig.

Gibraltar

As is well known, the Rock provides the foundation for many offshore banking services. It is even possible to form a private company there for a few hundred pounds and avoid death and inheritance taxes by buying your Spanish property in the company's name. Although the Spanish Tax Office (*Hacienda*) is making grumbling noises about this practice, assuring a future tax on property bought in this manner, it has yet to be passed and implemented.

At the moment Remington Knight Associates of the United States maintain it has the solution in forming a US corporation for the offshore company ownership of Spanish properties. Spain does not have a double-taxation avoidance treaty with the United States unlike Gibraltar and other tax-havens.

If you are interested in saving as much capital as you can, you will obtain many pointers by visiting Gibraltar, perusing its Press and the invaluable *Sur in English*.

INVESTING IN SPAIN

Gibraltar is awash not only with many concerns anxious to help you invest your money, but also the inevitable scandals. Again the local Press will give many details but the locals themselves will be able to give you the best advice.

Spain has its own fair share of investment companies. These have become reduced in number since a watch-dog committee was formed a few years ago to monitor all transactions and especially those which offer a larger than normal profit margin. This committee is called the CNMV (*Comisión Nacional del Mercado de Valores*). It has to approve take-over bids, share deals and practices.

WATCHING THE EXCHANGE RATES

If you are planning to retire to Spain you should take full account of the fluctuations in the value of currencies. Some retired people have been forced to return to their home countries owing to this unpleasant surprise. You must choose a currency which is likely to maintain its international value. The Swiss franc heads the list, resisting the rise of the peseta against many currencies. The US dollar may be the worst having started at 60 pesetas each, rising to a peak of 220 pesetas each and now falling past the 160 peseta mark.

USING CHEQUES

Whether you are retiring to Spain, work there or are an occasional visitor, it is worth knowing the legislation concerning Spanish cheques (*talones*). The first line of a cheque must say '*por este cheque*'. An old *talón* without this phrase is invalid. The same applies to any cheque whose date is more than six months old. Post-dated cheques are paid on presentation. All dates must be written out in full in Spanish, i.e. *diez de diciembre*, not 10/12/9x.

It is a common sight in Spanish banks to see people turned away because there is not sufficient in the account to cover the cheque, even though the law says that the bank must pay out whatever is left in the account.

If your cheque book is stolen you should inform your bank immediately so that your account may be frozen. As a precaution, many people carry only one cheque or perhaps two and hide away their cheque book at home.

If you make a cheque out to *al portador* it means 'the Bearer' and the cheque may be cashed by anyone. So make sure it goes into your account and nobody else's.

USING THE SPANISH *LETRA*

Any consideration of finance would be incomplete without explaining the *letra*, a word heard universally in Spain.

A *letra* is a form of hire purchase. It means if you buy a refrigerator and decide to pay a deposit of a third of its value and the rest on hire purchase you will have to sign maybe a dozen *letras* to the rest of the value agreed. You used to be able to complain about faulty goods by halting payment on the *letras* but as these days most people exchange the *letras* for a loan with a merchant bank or some other finance, the withholding of payments would not have the desired effect. In fact, if you do not have the funds available to cover the payment you may receive a *letra protestada* from your bank, forcing you to pay the amount and extra costs. This is a very common occurrence these days, so it does not cause the alarm it may have done fifty years ago.

One word of caution. If you sign a *letra* it becomes a personal debt. If you sign one for any concern make sure that concern becomes liable for the debt, otherwise you could find the debt of a housing development, cargo ship or car round your neck. This could be even more worrying than the *hipoteca* on property mentioned in Chapter 4.

FINAL POINTS TO PONDER

These are a few questions you should ask yourself if you are considering retirement in Spain.

- Is it worth forming an off-shore company in Gibraltar?

- Would a family trust based in Andorra suit my purposes better?

- Would Spanish or other national investment funds give the best results?

- How will currency fluctuations affect my plans?

- Which credit cards will suit me best in Spain?

- Can I adapt to Spanish cheque usage or lack of it?

- Would it be better to have my pension paid into a foreign bank and use Eurocheques to withdraw it?

- Which particular professional advisers should I choose?

8

Becoming Wise

This chapter aims to help you integrate with Spanish society by learning about the language, the education system, the social customs, the nature and culture of the people themselves. In fact, a minor exercise in philology.

UNDERSTANDING THE EDUCATION SYSTEM

The Spanish have always recognised the value of a good education. Spain has some of the oldest established universities like the *Universidad Complutense* in Alcalá de Henares, founded in 1499. In those days graduation was celebrated in style: the results would be read to the general public in the forecourt of this university; those who had passed the examinations would be carried through the main entrance by their companions: those who had failed would be taken out through the back door, placed in a cart and conveyed round the town to be ridiculed. This university was also the first to admit women. Dona Maria Isidra Quintana Guzmán y de la Cerda graduated in 1785 and was nicknamed the Doctora de Alcalá.

These days education is taken just as seriously and the Spanish are usually prepared to make considerable sacrifices to ensure their children receive a proper education. Private education can be very expensive and is often run or controlled by the Catholic Church. State education is compulsory from the ages of 6 until 16 and is free.

However, as in so many countries at the moment, education is the subject of much discussion and new proposals. Legislation in 1990 established a new education system, summarised below.

LOGSE – THE NEW LEGISLATION FOR EDUCATION

LOGSE stands for *Ley Organica de Ordención Géneral del Sistema Educativo* (Fundamental Law for the General Organisation of the Education System). It was passed on 3 October 1990.

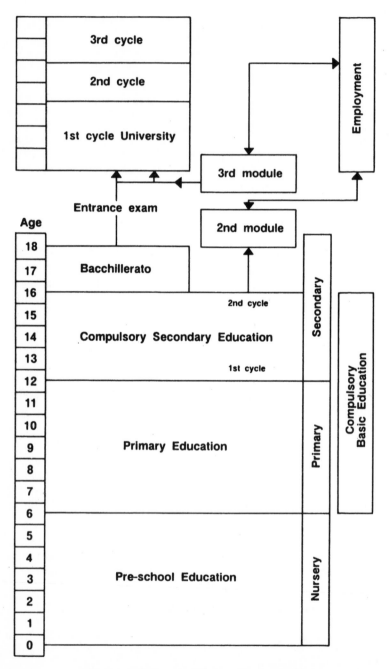

Fig. 10.   Spain's education system (LOGSE).

Private education is intended to run side by side with state eduction and enhance and augment it. Greater stress is being given to adult literacy and indeed education for all. Careers counselling is being introduced. Religion is no longer a mandatory subject; ethics will be taught instead to non-Catholics.

New universities are being established and new courses introduced. It is now possible to learn art, history, food science and technology, industrial design and there is greater stress on culture: ballet, theatre, painting, etc.

Although educational experts were consulted, the introduction of LOGSE has not met with an enthusiastic response from teaching staff. Full implementation of LOGSE to the third stage of education is not planned until the end of the century.

Figure 10 summarises the new system, and Figure 11 compares the new system with the old. The standard of basic education will be raised by extending the length of time a student attends school before the choice is made between *bachillerato* and vocational training.

Infant education
Extended to 6 years of age, with two cycles: up to 3 years of age and from 3 to 6 years of age. This cycle is not compulsory. However, the central Administration co-ordinates the number of school places for infant education offered by the different public administrations. There is a recognition of the educative value of this period, the aim being to contribute to the physical and personal development of the child. Regulations lay down the conditions which are to be complied with by centres offering infant education.

Primary education
Primary education consists of six academic courses from 6 to 12 years organised in three cycles of two years for each cycle. This is a compulsory educational cycle and is free of charge.

Its aim is to promote the socialisation of the students, encourage their incorporation to the culture and contribute to the progressive autonomy of action in its environment. Teaching methods have a personal character and are adapted to the different learning capacities of each student.

Students with extra intelligence are now given special attention and facilities.

The new system	(LOGSE)	Age	Substitutes (law of 1970)
Infant education	3–5	—	
Primary education	1°	6–7	1st EGB
First cycle	2°	7–8	2nd EGB
Primary education	3rd	8–9	3rd EGB
Second cycle	4th	9–10	4th EGB
Primary education	5th	10–11	5th EGB
Third cycle	6th	11–12	6th EGB
Secondary education	1st	12–13	7th EGB
First cycle	2nd	13–14	8th EGB
Secondary education	3rd	14–15	1st of BUPA/1st from FPI
Second cycle	4th	15–16	2nd of BUP/2nd from FPO
Bachillerato	1st	16–17	3rd BUP 1st of FPII of Special Studies Course for access from FPI to FPII
Bachillerato	2nd	17–18	COU 2nd of FPII of Special Studies. 1st of FPI from General Org.

Note: EGB = Basic General Education, FP = Vocational Training, BUP = Secondary School, COU = Pre-University Course.

Fig. 11. LOGSE (the new education system) and corresponding parts of old system.

Principal innovations include:

- the learning of one **foreign language** from the age of eight with specialised teachers
- specialised teachers for **physical education**
- progressive incorporation of specialised teachers in **musical education**

- education more adapted to the special and diversified **needs** of children

- a minimum of 25 students per classroom (except in special needs because of schooling).

Secondary education

Compulsory secondary education
Statutory secondary education is a compulsory and free of charge cycle, which includes four courses corresponding with the actual two final courses of EGB (7th and 8th) and the two first courses of the old secondary education (1st and 2nd of BUP or FP). It is divided in two cycles of two years each: the first cycle from 12 to 14 years of age, and the second cycle: from 14 to 16 years of age.

The objective of the design of this educational level aims basically at extending compulsory education to the age of 16, in this way levelling with the initial labour age of any Spanish citizen and balancing the Spanish educational system with those of the other countries of the European Union.

All students who pass the primary education stage have direct access to statutory secondary education. Any students who do not pass the primary stage will have to repeat their final year.

Students who pass the first cycle are given access to the second. Again, any students who do not pass the first cycle will have to repeat one or two years.

Innovations at this stage include the following:

- The average per school unit is 30 students

- The tuition in this stage is of a comprehensive character

- The use of options is established, which is progressive towards the end of the stage, thus allowing the student to choose some of the subjects of each course.

- Departments for Orientation are established with monitors – a psychologist or a pedagogue – and two or three teachers for support to the students and especially to those with special learning difficulties.

- Technological subjects have been introduced as part of basic vocational training and as a general necessary learning field for all students.

- Teaching methods are adapted to the characteristics of each student, showing them how to learn by themselves and how to work in groups.

- Evaluation, which is continuous and integrated, will allow the students who have not reached the objectives of the first cycle to repeat one year, as well as one more year in any of the courses of the Second Cycle.

- Personalised tuition is one of the landmarks of the new educational system. Some students, because of their personal character, need more specific attention and resources. A programme for integration to secondary education and programmes for syllabus diversification have been started.

At the end of statutory secondary education the students will receive the qualification of **Graduate in Secondary Education**, if they have passed this stage satisfactorily. To those not passing this stage, a **Certificate** will be given, in which the courses followed and the qualifications achieved in each subject will be stated. The qualification of **Graduate in Secondary Education** gives entry conditions to:

- Bachillerato LOGSE

- intermediate vocational training cycles.

Social warranty programmes
Those students between 16 and 21 years of age who have not reached the objectives of statutory secondary education and do not hold any qualifications in vocational training, have the possibility of enrolling in some courses of the social warranty programme, where the emphasis is on vocational and practical training.

Bachillerato (non-compulsory upper secondary education)
The new Bachillerato has the following features:

- Part of secondary education.

- Two academic courses.

- Number of students per group is 35.

- Gives to students a human and intellectual maturity and knowledge and abilities which allow them to carry out their social functions with competence and responsibility.

- Incorporation to basic vocational training allows the student to outline various training routes towards the vocational qualification.

- Carried out in 4 modalities, which ensures a basic training of vocational character and a personal maturity which facilitates the transition of the students to the active life. These modalities are: art; health and environmental sciences; humanities and social sciences; technology. Each of these modalities are angled towards certain university studies.

Successful completion of the Bachillerato gives entry conditions to:

- advanced level vocational training cycles
- university, through access exams.

The new vocational training
The new vocational training aims to equip students for an environment of rapid social and technological change. A further objective is to bring vocational training up to European Union standards.

Vocational training is defined as the learning of those subjects that enable the student to carry out competently the various professions. Apart from specific vocational training, all students from six years of age until the end of any Bachillerato, receive **basic vocational training**.

The university system
A process of reform and modernisation of university education was begun in 1987, with the following four objectives:

- **actualising** the training and knowledge which are given in Spanish universities

- **flexibility** in the training given

- **linking** university and society by matching training to social needs

- **adapting** the advanced level training system to the requirement of European Union directives.

The Spanish university system includes 47 public universities, 5 private universities and 4 universities of the Catholic Church.

The universities are autonomous and offer their own academic qualifications which could be of two different types:

- official qualifications which are valid throughout Spain
- qualifications which are established by the particular university.

The official qualifications are established by the Government by proposal from the Council of the Universities. In the same manner, the Government by proposal from the Council of the Universities establishes the general proper directions of these qualifications, i.e. the minimum 'common core subjects' to be included in the study plans.

The universities elaborate and approve their own study plans which include, apart from the common core subjects, the compulsory subjects of the university, optional subjects for the students, and subjects chosen by the students.

MAKING USE OF THE EDUCATION SYSTEM

In general, foreign residents seem to avail themselves of Spanish nursery education and, to lesser extent, primary education. Young children easily pick up languages. Parents of older children usually prefer to make other arrangements for secondary education. This could be because it is so different from the British system. Spanish ministers and VIPs frequently send their children to foreign universities simply because the courses are so long in Spain.

Many British schools operate in Spain. You can obtain a list from:

National Association of British Schools in Spain (NABSS), Avda, Ciudad de Barcelona 110-esc, 3/5° D, 28007 Madrid. Tel: 91 552 05 16.

British Council, Paseo General Martinez Campos 31, 28010 Madrid. Tel: 91 337 35 00.

LEARNING THE LANGUAGE

Adults are not immune to the process of education and it is recommended that you should attempt to learn *castellano* if you intend to reside in Spain for any length of time. Many discover that the time and expense of a course in spoken Spanish proves a very sound investment. It will certainly enhance your enjoyment of Spain.

Castellano is a very easy language to learn because it is written phonetically. Once you have mastered the basic vowel and consonant sounds you will have no problems reading or writing Spanish. Many of the words share common roots with other European languages but the pronunciation may be a little different. Once you have learned the language a whole new world of communication will be open to you. Whatever their faults, the Spanish are never short of words. Here is a list of idioms, very useful to know and not always covered in language courses.

Useful Spanish idioms

pegar la hebra	to have a long conversation
a bombo y platillo	with much display, ostentation
abrir calle	open a way through a crowd
a cosa hecha	certain to be done, a success
a cuerpo de rey	live like a king
a la vejez, viruelas	an old person behaving like a youngster
al grano	to the point, don't be vague
borrón y cuenta nueva	finish one subject and start another
cabeza de turco	scapegoat
como aguas de mayo	something very welcome
de Madrid al cielo	after Madrid, only heaven is better
Dios los cria y ellos se juntan	birds of a feather flock together

echar leña al fuego	add new contention to a dispute
echar pestes	to pick a person to pieces
echar una cana al aire	take time off, enjoy yourself, let your hair down
el gozo en un pozo	lose hope of fulfilling a desire
el saber no ocupar lugar	knowledge or education is always useful
es el cuento de nunca acabar	it's a long story
estar a dos velas	to be broke (financially)
esta sin blanca	to be broke (financially)
estar hecho un brazo de mar	to compliment a female on her appearance regardless of age
gato por liebre	to pass off inferior goods or services as high quality
haber gato encerrado	to have an ulterior motive
hablar por los codos	to talk non-stop
hacer pucheros	to weep like a small child
hallar la horma de su zapato	to find just what you want
hay más días que longanizas	there's plenty of time
hecha la ley, hecha la trampa	those who make the law also provide loopholes
ir con pies de plomo	to be very careful
ir de capa caída	on a downward path
la pobreza no esta reñida con la limpieza	poverty does *not* mean one is dirty
loco de atar	really crazy, enough to be tied down
mandar a freír espárragos	to tell someone to get lost, jump in the lake
meter la pata	to put your foot in it
nadie diga de este agua no beberé	don't say it won't happen to you

ni fu ni fa	(an expression of indifference)
no es santo de mi devoción	a person with whom one is not at ease
no llegar la sangre al río	the fight did not become serious
no se ganó Zamora en una hora	Rome wasn't built in a day
no tener donde caerse muerte	very poor
para muestra un botón	a small sample of the whole (bad) truth
pasar las de Caín	bad experience(s)
pedir peras al ormo	ask for the impossible
quedar compuesta y sin novio	to be left at the altar
sacar de quicio	to make someone wild, see red
salvarse por los pelos	escape by the skin of one's teeth
ser una cosa el pan nuestro de cada día	an everyday occurrence
subirselo a uno el pavo	to blush like a lobster
tal para cual	one as untrustworthy as the other
tener buen diente	to be a good eater, have a good appetite
tener la sarten por el mango	to be in the commanding position
tener mala pata	to have bad luck
tener malas pulgas	to have bad motives, disagreeable
tomar el pelo a uno	to pull one's leg
una de cal y otra de arena	one as good as the other is bad
ver las orejas al lobo	to see another's bad intentions
vivir de la sopa boba	live at someone else's expense
viva la Pepa!	to live without worrying about the cost, to blazes with everyone else

If you can learn just a few of these, they will help you to integrate more quickly into the Spanish way of life, as does learning the language properly. It makes it easier for you to be accepted, even by those who are fluent in English.

Perhaps the only people who do not need to know any Spanish are the VIPs in multinational companies. They are surrounded by polyglot staff and are sheltered from the normal requirements of everyday life. For them Spain is another step on the corporate career ladder, as they commute to and from HQ on transatlantic flights in the near stratosphere. However, for ordinary mortals who live at lower altitudes a working knowledge of *castellano* is a must.

Some foreigners live in ghettos with little or no contact with the natives. They are missing a great deal. You should take every opportunity to fraternise in a country where there is little racial feeling and foreigners are welcome.

Unfortunately, many do miss out on the delights of Spanish life. A recently published survey reports that some 70 per cent of foreigners are unable to maintain a normal conversation in Spanish. It is even more sad that over 20 per cent do not believe it necessary to learn Spanish. These people live in many of the *urbanizaciones* along the coasts. These have become foreign colonies and virtual ghettos. If you should wander into a café in one of these places and ask for *café con leche* the request may be ignored. If you ask for a *café au lait* or *reversée* you will receive quick service.

When you are buying a property it is a good idea to find out what nationalities predominate in the area. You will find learning Spanish considerably easier than Swedish if you want to understand your neighbours.

Spanish courses

You will have to decide which course suits you best. There is an endless variety. Some courses in schools are available on a national basis like Berlitz, Mangold, Assimil and so on. Many others are regional or confined to one city. Again the locals' knowledge will direct you to the best. All sorts of methods are available. One practical tip is to listen to the language as much as possible. Use the radio, play cassettes in your car. The sound structure will become familiar even if the meaning does not. Once you have established a basic knowledge and you are living in Spain you will be able to appreciate many of the social customs.

GETTING TO KNOW THE SOCIAL CUSTOMS

Those who become acquainted with the basic social functions in Spain are showing real wisdom, even though there are regional variations as usual.

Births, deaths and other occasions

These usually involve four wheels and are regular get-togethers.

Baptism is a social occasion even for the most modern-minded mums and dads. First Communions usually take place in April and May, when the ten-year-olds take their first communion in the Catholic Church. There will be a real feast which will be paid for by even the most Socialist father.

At weddings the bride usually wears a long white gown. It is the opportunity for another feast with dancing and drinking lasting for many hours. A present is a social nicety, and a necessity for any close relative. Total participation will be required of you whatever your religious convictions. The customs of the Catholic Church still prevail even though only 20 per cent of Spaniards are practising Catholics. These celebrations are a costly business for the family.

Funerals are also an expensive affair. Bearing in mind the high death toll on the roads it is perhaps a wise precaution to obtain insurance to cover such costs.

When a friend or acquaintance makes his last journey it is considered a very serious omission if you do not go to pay your last respects or, to give it the correct Spanish term, *dar el pésame*. You must greet the family and friends by shaking hands with them all and saying that you are extremely sorry. You may say such things as 'I'm sorry (*Lo siento*)' or '*Les doy(damos) mi (nuestro) más sentido pésame*' or '*vengo (venimos) a darles el*' or '*la (las) acompaño (acompañamos) en el sentimento*'. The words in brackets are used if you are not going on your own. The visible expression of grief is considered good form too, as is weeping in public, for many reasons.

Happy events

For those of us who believe firmly in the resurrection of Jesus Christ, his resurrection gives us hope of a future life, which helps in times of funerals and accidents. While grief should be publicly shown on these occasions, when Christmas comes it is a happy time for celebration over an extended period.

The family usually gathers together for Christmas Eve dinner with all the traditional trimmings of roast sea bream, roast lamb and all types of sea food, including king prawns and scampi and so on. A night of dancing and merry-making is traditional. Although this custom is dying out, if you have Spanish neighbours it is advisable to ask them what their plans are for Christmas Eve. It may be a case of 'if you can't beat them, join them'. The feast continues throughout Christmas Day, when you can wish everyone '*Feliz Navidad*' (Happy Christmas).

The same applies to New Year's Eve. Gifts are exchanged on the Day of the Three Kings (*Los Tres Reyes*), 6 January, or Epiphany. On this day there will be processions through the towns and cities with the Three Kings. Things are changing though; the most modern talk of Papa Noel and 25 December and give presents then. These are considered to be national customs. The regional ones are the *fiestas* which in the north consist typically of funfair entertainment, sports and competitions, and dancing. Generally when you have seen a *fiesta* in Asturias, you have seen a *fiesta* in Galicia or Navarra or other regions. On the Mediterranean coast there will be traditional mock battles between Moors and Christians. In Andalucia there are religious festivals when the images are carried through the streets, or processions are made into the country to some small church (*ermita*). Generally a good time will be had by all, especially if some public weeping can be included. This is just as much an expression of happiness as of sadness in the real Spain.

LIVING WITH THE SPANISH

When your studies of language, local idioms and everyday customs are progressing, you will start to get used to living with the Spanish and find that they are a friendly gregarious people who know how to make strangers feel at home. The family events are times when you can let your hair down and the local *fiestas* help you feel part of the scenery. Apart from these events there are family get togethers and ordinary invitations, all happy events. The social reserve which exists in other countries is almost unknown in Spain.

No class barriers

It is a common sight to see the workmen who are improving the pavement in front of a high class bar, having a drink on the house and being accepted quite naturally. They may not, of course, be quite so welcome at the golf club! Even in a five star hotel, you may use the wrong knife and fork without incurring the grim silence this would cause in countries nearer the North Pole.

Family life

Family life is still strong in Spain in various degrees. If you participate in it you may be surprised at the warmth which exists among family members. Wedding anniversaries and such events are well planned and the resulting conversation over the well-cooked meal may last long after eating has finished. In the summer, many families like to go to special sites where fires can be lit so that the male members may show their proficiency in cooking *paella*, and maintaining the wood fire at the correct temperature. This makes a pleasant day in the countryside.

If you are contemplating marriage, you will doubtless have an able teacher to educate you in the customs but for retired people and others, it is useful to know that many families still operate as a unit. Even in modern families, parents are still respected. They may still expect their unmarried daughters to be home by 22.00 or 23.00 except in special cases.

Many families still have three or more children but the trend is towards two. It is also becoming more usual to plan a family rather than attempting to prove how *macho* the bridegroom is by producing a baby in the shortest possible time. In some cases it used to be 'just in time or born in the belfry'. This is rare these days since abortions (though controversial) have been made available.

Socialising

This can take many forms, from the brief invitation to have a drink in the local bar – where all the family is at home – to spending a day or the weekend in the country cottage/house/flat which is the extension of many a Spanish town house.

The late evening meal is well known. So if you are invited to dinner, the repast will probably start about 22.00 and finish at midnight, or an hour or two later if you are dining in a restaurant. Figure 12 gives you an idea of the kind of menu you may expect at a restaurant.

Antigua Cocina
Mozárabe de Córdoba

SALMOREJO	750
CARDOS CON ALMEJAS Y CAMBAS	1.350
REVUELTO DEL SIGLO XI	950
CAZUELA DE VERDURAS CON CORDERO	1.200
BERENGENAS CON PERDIZ A MANZANA	1.200
MERLUZA «AL ANDALUS»	1.500
RAPE CON PASAS DE CORINTO Y PIÑON	1.500
1/2 PERDIZ «ZIRYAB»	900
CORDERO A LA MIEL	1.450
RIÑONADA DE CORDERO CON ALMENDRA PICADA Y PIMIENTA NEGRA	1.800
ESCALOPINES CON SETAS AL ROMERO	900
SUSPIRO DE ALMANZOR	500
DELICIAS DEL C. ROJO	500
HOJALDRE AL LIMON Y NARANJA	600

Entradas y
Entremeses

JAMON SERRANO	1.500
CAÑA DE LOMO DE JABUGO	1.300
SALMON AHUMADO «NORUEGO»	1.600
ENSALADA DE SALMON Y ANGULAS	2.200
SURTIDO DE AHUMADOS	1.500
BONITO DE BERMEO ENCEBOLLADO CON PIMIENTOS AL SARMIENTO	950
ESPARRAGOS FRIOS DOS SALSAS	850
ENSALADA ANDALUZA	475
SALMON MARINADO AL CULANTRO	1.600
MUSSE DE ESPARRAGOS AL APIO	750
QUESO MANCHEGO AÑEJO CURADO EN ACEITE	650

I.V.A. NO INCLUIDO

Cardenal Herrero, 28. Telfs.: 47 53 75 - 47 80 01 - 14003 Córdoba

Sopas

GAZPACHO DE ALMENDRAS	700
GAZPACHO CORDOBES	600
SOPA DEL MAR	900
SOPA DE CAMPIÑA A LA HIERBABUENA CON JAMON	750

Las Verduras

NUESTRO REVUELTO	900
ALCACHOFAS A LA MONTILLANA	850
LOS PIMIENTOS DEL PIQUILLO RELLENOS CON MARISCOS Y PESCADO	1.050

Aves y Caza

CONEJO EN PEPITORIA	850
MUSLOS DE CAPON RELLENOS AL FOIE-GRAS	950
PERDIZ ENCEBOLLADA	1.650
MAGRET DE OCA	1.700

Pescados

PEZ DE ESPADA AL HORNO	900
LOMOS DE MERLUZA CANTABRICA CON ANGULAS	2.200
CAZUELA DE PESCADO AL PEDRO XIMENEZ	1.500
LENGUADO AL VINAGRE BLANCO (S/ mercado y peso)	
RAPE CON SALMON AHUMADO EN SALSA VERDE	1.950
SALMON FRESCO AL VINO DEL DUERO	1.700

Las Carnes

RABOS DE TORO A MI ESTILO	975
ENTRECOT DE CEBON	1.600
CHULETAS DE CORDERO	1.450
SOLOMILLO A LA PARRILLA	1.500
PIERNA DE CORDERO AL HORNO	1.500
CHULETAS DE LALIN	1.750

Los Vinos de la Casa

VALDEPEÑAS	450
VEGA DEL DUERO 83	1.300

Cardenal Herrero, 28. Telfs.: 47 53 75 - 47 80 01 - 14003 Córdoba

Fig. 12.   Sample Spanish restaurant menu.
(Please note a wide variation in prices exists.)

It is also the pleasant custom for the entire family to be present at the table, youngest to oldest. Conversation is usually loud and sustained, no awkward British silences. You may almost have to shout to get a comment in at the right moment. The Spaniards are expert at talking and eating at the same time. Both are enjoyed and taken seriously as arts to be mastered, an essential part of one's education.

Etiquette
If you intend staying with a Spanish family remember:

- Breakfast will usually be light, lunch and dinner/supper plentiful.

- A mid-morning snack or mid-afternoon tea (*merienda*) is often served. This will help tide you over until the next proper meal.

- Hospitality may be expansive. If you are invited to a family feast it is bad form not to enjoy it to the full.

- Special occasions result in special meals, and, again, the host will be offended if you do not partake of every dish.

Family feasts may include hors d'oeuvres, soup, fish, meat and a dessert. However, if you are eating *merienda*, dish after dish of delicacies may appear, all to be sampled and enjoyed.

Please remember that it is the custom for any guest or guests to take a gift for the *creatora* of the coming repast. This may be flowers or more normally a kilo of *pasteles* (small cakes) which everyone may enjoy with the coffee at the end of the meal. A bottle of good wine also makes an acceptable gift.

If you have Spanish neighbours you may invite them for coffee, then perhaps *merienda* and later, meals or outings if you become really friendly. There is little resistance to foreigners except in the most isolated parts of Spain. On the Costa del Sol, Majorca and parts of the Canaries the importance of foreigners in raising living standards is fully appreciated and you should be made to feel welcome. The mayors (*alcaldes*) of some towns make special arrangements for residents who are natives of other countries.

Tapas
These have become so well known that books have been written on the subject and bars named after them. This excellent Spanish

custom is now becoming international. For newcomers to Spain, *tapas* are delicious morsels of all sorts of delicacies. They are served before the lunch hour as an accompaniment to the drinks you may order before having lunch. Originally *tapas* were pieces of highly spiced sausage (*chorizo*) served with a *copita* (small glass) of wine. These days an extensive range of goodies is on offer. This is one of the many pleasant features of Spain which may be enjoyed by the whole family on their Sunday outing.

After *tapas* the typical family returns to a hearty lunch so if you have been invited along it is as well not to have eaten too many *tapas*.

Lunchtime tertulias

There is no danger of a spider attack if you are invited to one of these. It is a daily meeting of old friends in their favourite café. Current topics will be discussed in a friendly atmosphere. In the upper class restaurants of Madrid's *calle de Alcalá*, it takes on the appearance of a traditional ceremony. Special tables are reserved for the same (normally) select group every day. The permanent nature of these *tertulias* in the same café at the same table with the same participants underlines a characteristic of many Spaniards, the love of tradition and retention of old habits. Although it may be the 'in thing' to be an atheistic politician, a Spaniard would probably never dream of allowing his child to remain unbaptised. The same is true of holidays. Many families own and return year after year to the same flat or chalet in a particular seaside resort.

Wine

You will find vineyards in almost every part of Spain, except the most humid. Wine has long been glorified in Spanish literature, exported in billions of litres and enjoyed by millions of tourists as well as the Spanish themselves. Curiously enough, although wine can be bought almost anywhere at any time, drunken behaviour is less frequently seen in public than in those countries where the purchase of wine is restricted. This does not mean that there are no alcoholics in Spain. Alcoholism is often described as a major problem, but it applies also to the foreign population. On the Costa del Sol, the 'sun-downer' is often followed by the 'sun-riser' and continues through the day and night.

Good wine should never be abused, however, and there are plenty of good wines to choose from.

UNDERSTANDING THE SPANISH CHARACTER

It is difficult to write about the 'typical' Spaniard, considering all the regional differences and the great changes that have taken place over the last twenty to thirty years. The younger generation have become more and more preoccupied with the material offerings of life. They may spend up to the very last peseta, meaning a considerable combined income in many modern marriages. At Christmas the couples may be several pay cheques ahead of their actual income with credit cards stretched to the limit.

Amando de Miguel observes in his book *Los Españoles:* '*Quéde-monos como somos, un pueblo viejo, teatrero, tierno, socarrón y alborotador.*' (We remain as we are, a people who have ancient roots, and are theatrical, tender in feelings, ironical and boisterous.) After a five course luncheon in a five star restaurant where you may have had to shout to make yourself heard across the table, you may feel the last adjective could be put more forcibly. In fact, *alborotador* may be translated as noisy, turbulent, rebellious or mischief-making. All of these describe the Spanish character and you should take it into account in your dealings with them.

Señor don Julio Caro-Baroja, a Spanish historian, linguist and anthropologist, opines, 'I have always believed that a Spaniard is not an individualist, but a *personalist*, which is different. He is a man who concentrates so much on himself, that he only knows about himself. At the same time, his impetus is such that it seems that no one else exists, in a way which is frightening.' This argument is used by some people to explain why a driver may not use his indicators – everyone should know where he is going!

Some traits and trends

In spite of the faults in the Spanish character in general, *extremismo, celos o enviadia* (jealousy or envy), the saving grace of the Spanish is their gregariousness and hospitality.

The hospitality is open-hearted and even excessive. The discussion over who should pay the bill for a round of drinks can be heated. Each side claims his right to pay – so unlike other countries.

The café habit is firmly implanted in Spain. Most people have a favourite place for morning coffee, lunches out, evening meals and so on. That place becomes a kind of extension to the home.

The entire family will be there from the very youngest to the very oldest. Conversations may go on way past midnight in the summer and, as mentioned, there will be little sign of drunkenness.

It is difficult to be lonely in Spain. If you stop to cross the road, a stranger may start a conversation on some current topic, and ask your opinion. The same friendliness is evident everywhere, from the four-year-old who asks you the time to the friendly barman or waiter who becomes almost one of the family when you frequent a particular café or restaurant.

The Spanish have a naturally optimistic outlook on life, and try to enjoy it to the full. The foreigner is quickly accepted if he fits into their way of life and does not expect them to change to suit him.

Amando de Miguel has a theory that the outward cheerfulness of the Spaniard is designed to hide an internal melancholy and quotes a popular song: '*Cuando el español canta, no está contento, es que, cantando, ahoga su sufrimiento.*' (When the Spaniard sings, he is not content, he's drowning his sorrow by singing.) Whatever the reason, the outward expression of the people of Spain is cheerfulness. While people of other races seem, at times, to be waiting for death as a happy release, the average Spaniard seems intent on getting the most out of life whether it be cutting meat in the market, serving in a bar, driving a taxi or running one of the largest national companies.

The tolerance of foreigners is another attractive Spanish trait. In the country, the sole English inhabitant in a hamlet may be called *el francés* (the Frenchman). To many older people all foreigners are Frenchmen and their habits are tolerated quite well.

Business life
To counter-balance the appeal of hospitality, team spirit and industry you will find the average Spaniard unwilling to write letters – everything is done by telephone or fax – and, worst of all, late.

The Spaniard may talk admiringly of British seriousness, formality and punctuality, but this is all theory. In Spain punctuality is almost a vice and if you arrive at the office at the right time for an appointment or earlier you may be made to feel very uncomfortable. You are expected to arrive about half an hour late, make a few comments on the terrible state of the traffic and the impossibility of parking, and then get down to work. This may be followed by a long but excellent lunch lasting from about 14.30 until 17.30 after which most people go home.

Regional characteristics

All generalisations are dangerous. Although Andalusians are popularly supposed to enjoy *fiestas*, song and dance, your neighbours from that region may be hardworking, clean and respectful, characteristics not attributed in general to people from the eight southernmost provinces.

However, allowing for those exceptions which prove the rule, you will find that the people in the north tend to be hearty eaters, good hosts, more industrious and better educated than their southern counterparts and more European in some respects. Of course, the northern peoples have their faults too. The people of Galicia, Cantabria, Asturias and the Basque Country have a liking for too much wine which results in unruly behaviour.

In Valencia and other eastern provinces where fruit has been grown for centuries, the people have a reputation for loving *fiestas*, being as tight with money as the Scots, and being as clean as the French. Andalucía is the fun region, symbolised by the Costa del Sol, one of the wealthiest areas in Spanish territory – and where work never seems to be taken too seriously. A full description of each of the seventeen provinces may be found in *Time Off In Spain and Portugal* by Teresa Tinsley. *Berlitz Blueprint Spain* is another good guide.

9

Holidaying in Spain

The scenery in the Iberian Peninsula is as varied as the types of transport available. If you are not in a hurry you could take a donkey taxi in Mijas, Costa del Sol. There is a boom in regional airlines and jetfoils cut journey times between the Canary Islands, crossing the Straits of Gibraltar and in the Balearic Islands.

Trains may prove their utility by luxury trips to help you become better acquainted with Spain, links overnight with Paris or (down the price scale) day trips. AVE means bird in Spanish but this 'bird' will never fly as it is the acronym for the new Spanish high speed train, which first ran in 1992 the year of the Barcelona Olympics and the Seville World Exhibition. The train will eventually shuttle between these two cities via Madrid at 300 kmph. Additional railway routes are planned to link into the European network (see Figure 13).

TRAVELLING BY AIR

Aviaco has been the Spanish domestic airline for a long time. It uses DC-9 and F-27 aeroplanes providing links between the smaller cities such as Vigo, Zaragoza, La Coruña and the main industrial centres. Some complain that there are too many airports in Spain so do not be surprised to find one not too far away from what you thought was quite an out of the way place.

The choice of airline is getting wider every day, especially following EU membership. As so many small airports and regional services are becoming available it is a good idea to make your travel agent check properly. His list may not be up to date. Here are some of the most recently announced airlines.

- *Air Europa* is the great newcomer with domestic flights, and regular and charter flights for international travel. Lots of *huge* special offers.

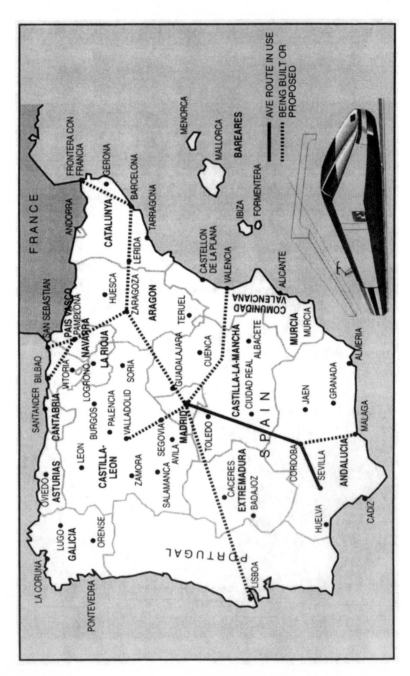

Fig. 13. The AVE high speed network.

- LAE (*Lineas Aéreas Extremeñas*). F-27s are used to link Madrid and Badajoz twice daily. There are plans to link in Barcelona, Bilbao, Valencia and other cities.

- Binter Canarias is a subsidiary of IBERIA and offers rapid connections to the Canary Islands using CN-235s, ATR-72s and DC-9s.

- Binter Mediterranea SA will link the Spanish mainland to the Balearic Islands and in the future North Africa, southern France and Italy. Already flies to Mellila in North Africa.

- Norjet flies from the airports of Vitoria and Bilbao to Europe and the rest of Spain. It is the first Basque airline.

- LAC (*Lineas Aereas Canarias*) uses MD-83s to ferry passengers from and around the Canary Islands to northern Europe.

- Air Sur began life in 1990 and was the first private line to be allowed to operate scheduled passenger services between Madrid and Valladolid. The service has since been extended to include Barcelona, Málaga and Seville.

- Baron von Wernitz plans complete coverage of the north coastal zone with his private airline, Wernitz Air. The company was formed in 1989 but ran into trouble. It should be functioning now.

- Binter Norte will cover the north coastal zone too *when* the authorisation has been processed.

It is likely that this list will grow since there are many other projects in hand and tourism is flourishing. While some airlines have folded, others succeed. *Air Europa* is an astounding success story in Spain and elsewhere. Newcomer 'Easy Jet' is also going well with very low prices.

TRAVELLING BY SEA

There are many useful ferries serving the islands and Africa. Jetfoil services are proving very popular with those who like to cut travelling time to a minimum and enjoy the sensation of travelling over the waves. And for those who like the idea of something exotic a transparent submarine is on order from Finland for use in the Balearics.

Jetfoil services

The papers greeted the advent of the first jetfoil in Spain with headlines such as 'The First European', 'Best In The World' and so on despite the fact that the jetfoil has been well known for decades. The services link Spanish ports, the Canary Islands and cross the Straits of Gibraltar from Algeciras to Ceuta. It is planned to serve Melilla too. These services are organised by *Compañía Trasmediterránea*.

Private services are also being developed. There is a summer only service from Denia on the Costa Blanca to Alicante and Ibiza. Other routes are under consideration. This also applies to Gibraltar. A jetfoil service could alleviate conditions in holiday periods. Immigrant Arab workers wishing to return home at these times create chaos. The Red Cross provides special temporary shelters for them. If you are planning to use this ferry crossing it is best to avoid July and August as an extremely long wait in trying circumstances is likely.

Sea ferries

The *Compañía (Cia) Trasmediterránea* has a long history of providing strategic connections between the Spanish mainland and the many islands under the Spanish flag. The fleet consists of about forty vessels which provide overnight services from Valencia to Majorca, Menorca, Ibiza and connections to Formentera. The same applies from Barcelona and the Balearic Islands, Cádiz and the Canary Islands, Algeciras and North Africa. In slack periods the ferries are used for cruises. If you have the time, a voyage can be more enjoyable than a flight and you can take your car too.

Owing to EU regulations and pressure from other companies, *Trasmediterránea* no longer has the monopoly on these services. Isnasa (*Isleña de Navegación*) is one rival. It operates four ferries providing eight services daily on the Algeciras–Ceuta route, six to Tangier and one from La Tarifa to Tangier.

Smaller companies ply between some ports but *Trasmediterránea* and Isnasa are the two main companies. They have now also been joined by *Ferrimaroc* plying between Almeria and Nador on Morocco's North African coast, as well as some other newcomers.

GOING OVERLAND ON THE TRAIN

Special day excursion trains

The State railway company, RENFE (*Red Nacional de Ferro-carriles Españoles*), introduced these in recent years in Madrid. They offer day trips to historical sites and the price includes the train fare, guides, and entrance fees to the places visited.

The star attraction is the excursion train to Aranjuez which was mentioned in Chapter 1. The line to Aranjuez was opened in 1850. The train you will take is steam-hauled using the original wooden rolling-stock. Hostesses in nineteenth-century costume will offer you strawberries and when you arrive the town band will serenade you.

Check with RENFE or local tourist information offices for other special train excursions.

Luxury trains

There are two extra special trains well worth the effort and expense. These are *El Andalus* and *El Transcantábrico*. They rival the Orient Express in the de luxe furnishings and fittings throughout.

El Andalus travels from Seville via Córdoba and Granada to Málaga and back again. If the entire trip is too expensive for you or you cannot spare so much time, it is possible to travel from Seville to Córdoba or Málaga to Seville. Great sensitivity to passenger comfort has been shown since the train makes an overnight stop in a siding to allow passengers to sleep instead of subjecting them to the discomforts of the Andalucian track. The route has also been specially designed to avoid as much as possible exposing passengers to the excessive heat of the Andalucian summer. The sleeping cars and suites were built in France in 1929 for the King of England to exacting standards, using expensive woods to create luxury decor. You too may enjoy living like royalty.

El Transcantábrico is a similar tourist train operating in the north and west, from Santiago de Compostela in Galicia to San Sebastián in the Basque region. Services operate from May to September, and prices for 1998 were:

Per person in double compartments	180,000 pesetas
Per person in single compartments	200,000 pesetas

IVA and SOV included. (Children under ten receive a 25% discount on the prices listed above).

Prices include:

- seven nights on board the train
- seven dinners and eight lunches with typical northern Spanish cuisine, including regional wines and coffee
- seven breakfasts on board (buffet)
- accompanying guide during the entire journey
- tour meals ordered in advance by train management
- musician who plays live music and parties at the pub-car
- all the excursions programmed on the itinerary, with entrance to museums, collegiate churches, casino, etc.
- bus during the entire voyage for sidetrips and restaurants

You can also hire *Transcantábrico* on a charter basis for business trips, pleasure, meetings, conferences or study groups.

Normal train services

There is a large variety of train services in Spain, ranging from the overnight luxury expresses to the railways of FEVE in the northern coastal region where wooden seats may still be found. Many improvements are being introduced. The European Union is making grants available on a massive scale and the State is underwriting losses so that new rolling-stock may be introduced.

There are suburban services from all the large cities, but you must not expect them to resemble services in the United Kingdom. A 30 kms journey from Madrid can and does take an hour, or more if the crews decide to strike. Striking is possible in the first six months of the year when the unions are negotiating the annual contract. Promises were continually being made to improve the *cercanías* (suburban services) and double level passenger carriages have been introduced. Some real improvements, have been made in recent years. However, business people still rarely commute to work. The car is preferred as a means of transport which helps to explain the massive traffic jams at peak times in Spanish towns and cities.

Most Spanish cities are linked by a variety of trains. You may take an intercity train to Valencia from Madrid or Barcelona to Zaragoza, travelling in air conditioned bliss. Services include waiters with trays of airline meals, buffet car open for the entire journey and entertainment such as television and video films. Again times could be improved and there are frequent delays. Intercity trains generally have first class and second class accommodation.

Prices vary widely but if you are a traveller on a low budget *literas* could be the answer. You pay for a bed in a compartment containing six berths. It is customary to sleep fully dressed as you cannot be sure whether you will be sharing the compartment with a beautiful American girl or an immigrant Arab worker. Conversation may be polyglot in character and may continue into the small hours. The prospect of a good night's sleep is small under these circumstances when you consider that someone is bound to snore.

The worst experience you will encounter is travelling on the Lusitania Express, overnight from Madrid to Lisbon. It is definitely an experience for the young at heart, not for those who value their creature comforts. The train reaches the Border in the very small hours of the morning when even the most inveterate talker has fallen asleep. The Portuguese frontier police and Customs officers proceed to invade the train and take over. They insist on seeing passports, ID cards and other documentation while the Customs officer interrogates you. The main aim seems to be to discourage you from visiting their country.

Of course you may opt for something more comfortable. First class travel in a seat is preferred by many and the seats are quite wide. The Wagons-lits are usually good, if you are affluent. Night travel in Andalucía is not to be recommended.

By contrast, the overnight train from Madrid to Paris is excellent. There is a wide range of services available from normal to luxury sleepers, restaurant car, showers, air conditioning.

The following accommodation is available on night trains. You pay your money and take your choice.

- Third class seat.

- *Literas* (sleeper bunk, six to a compartment).

- First class seat in an express.

- Normal sleeper.

- Luxury sleeper accommodation available on the Madrid–Paris route and a few others.

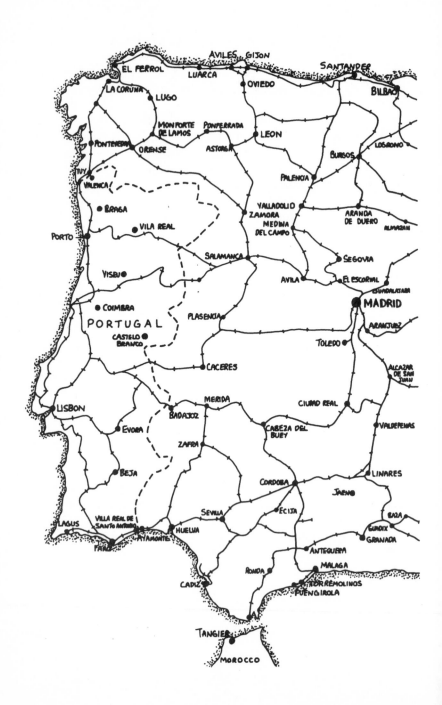

Fig. 14.   The Spanish railway system.

Locomotives available

The introduction of the AVE has enhanced rail travel in Spain. It is an extension of the TGV, high velocity units which operate in France and Germany, and uses the same gauge as the rest of Europe. The exact entry points into Spain have been a matter of heated discussion as both the Basques and Catalans wished to claim the privilege of the European linkage. The route from Seville to Madrid is now in operation (see Figure 13). It follows an entirely new route incorporating many tunnels. You should now enjoy rapid train travel to Seville. Before AVE, some expresses took 20 hours to travel from Barcelona to Seville.

Apart from this, the principal types of train that you will meet are the following.

- *Talgo*. This is a Spanish train on a triangular suspension provided by two wheels and a cantilever beam to the next coach. It is fast and usually quite comfortable. It has been sold to the USA and other countries, and in Spain is widely used by RENFE.

- *Ter*. This is a well built Italian train from FIAT. It is high off the ground, comfortable and has a suspension which allows you to write when travelling at high speed.

- *Electro-Tren*. This is a modern Spanish-built unit with video and cafeteria services. It is used on medium-length journeys.

- *Regional Express*. This consists of modern suburban coaches which should provide air conditioning and a few other amenities. They link Madrid with smaller provincial capitals.

- *Interurbano*. This is the Spanish equivalent of the suburban line. It has modern carriages, often crowded, and it usually runs to time, unless affected by strikes. Business commuters are increasingly encouraged to use these trains, as a more pleasant alternative to worsening traffic congestion, especially going into the cities, plus parking difficulties. (See also Chapter 10).

Ski trains

These are a novelty recently introduced by RENFE and there are two trips on offer. Remember to check the snow conditions with the Spanish ski and mountain association before you book either of these. Tel: 974 22 56 56.

The first is in the *Sierra Nevada*. The trip includes the return rail journey from Madrid to Granada, and accommodation in the Sierra Nevada, 30 kms from Granada. The ski slopes are between the altitudes of 2,100 and 3,470 metres above sea level and snow coverage continues late into the year. There are some twenty ski lifts for which you may obtain a season ticket. There are also instructors and classes and you are allowed the run of the resort with all its many amenities.

The other ski train is called the *Tren Blanco Estrella Pirineo*. It travels overnight from Madrid either to Jaca for the ski resorts of Candanchú and Astun or to Canfranca for the ski resorts of Formigal and Panticosa. There is a wide variety of train and hotel accommodation available. Jaca is a delightful little town which has an ice rink, ancient part and shops to supply all your needs. The hotels provide such large meals that it is advisable to eat only two meals a day. The same applies to resorts in Andorra.

The pros and cons of train travel
These are the advantages of train travel in Spain:

- You can visit interesting places relatively cheaply.

- You may obtain deep insights into the wealth of history exemplified by the physical survival of so many ancient buildings, documents and relics.

- The timetable is restful.

- The routes are specially planned to avoid the worst of the summer heat.

These are the disadvantages:

- Train travel may be very slow.

- The guides usually speak in Spanish – except on the most expensive excursions.

- Day trippers to Aranjuez must endure the wooden seats in the period rolling-stock.

- Toilets on many trains in Spain leave much to be desired.

FINDING ACCOMMODATION

Paradores Nacionales (PNs)

These State hotels are highly recommended for leisurely stays. Many are conversions of ancient historic buildings such as castles, palaces and monasteries. They offer modern comfort while preserving the atmosphere of the past. They are normally to four or five star standard and offer reasonable service with good cuisine. They will open your eyes to the wealth and might of Spain as a superpower of yesteryear. These buildings were built from the proceeds of some of the Spanish treasure galleons which arrived safely.

The Central Booking Office in Madrid (open from 09.30 until 13.30 and 16.30 until 19.30) can provide a booklet which lists almost all of the hotels in the chain with photographs. It is better to use the latest booklet as the less profitable hotels are sold or closed. Tel: 91 435 97 00.

It would be a millionaire's dream to stay in each and every one of these Paradors, from Monte Perdido in the Pyrenees in a beautiful snowy valley to the most western and southern on the island of La Gomera in the Canaries. You can decide whether to sleep in the same room as King Carlos V in the castle of Jarandilla de la Vera or dine in the students' hospice in the university of Alcalá de Henares.

Advantages of staying in a PN:

- You can book them in advance from any part of the world.

- There is a high standard of service and cleanliness.

- The cuisine is excellent, normally to international standards and caters for all tastes.

- The buildings are usually interesting but the facilities are modern.

- They are frequently located in beauty spots which are off the beaten track for tourists.

- There are polyglot receptionists who are anxious to make your stay pleasant.

- Many provide a restful environment and have a bird's eye view of the local surroundings.

Disadvantages of staying in a PN:

- They are expensive.

- At peak times of the year, bookings may be limited to three or four days.

- You usually need to book well in advance.

- Some of the modern PNs are right next to old cities and one feels that one of the old buildings should have been made available for conversion.

If you do not wish to stay in one of these Paradors or cannot afford it, you will find them open for refreshments from 8.00 until 22.00. The buffet breakfast is worth mentioning. You may choose from a selection of bacon, eggs, sausages, ham (York), a wide range of cold meats, cheeses, patés and Spanish ham (*serrano*). This is followed by all kinds of cake, fruits and fruit juices. You may go up as many times as you like. If the waitress seems a little worried she may want to know your room number (*¿'Su numero de habitación, por favor?'*). If you have only called in for breakfast you should reply, '*estamos de paso*', and ask for the bill when you have finished. About 1,300 pts each.

Spas

There are numerous spas scattered around the Iberian Peninsula. These will take you back to the last century with its leisurely way of life and treatments which range from a rest cure to a full medical programme controlled by doctors and staff. You may obtain information about these by writing to the address given in Chapter 5. Tel: 91 542 97 75.

There are several good spas in Aragón (the northern provinces of Zaragoza and Huesca) including the spectacular spa in the valley of the Panticosa, 1,600 metres above sea level. There are several three star hotels and good skiing. The spa is located 54 kms from Jaca and 97 kms from Huesca in the southern Pyrenees and is recommended.

Fourteen of Spain's seventeen regions have these spas which are still popular. It is a good idea to check them carefully before you go to stay there as they can be very expensive.

Hotel chains

Tourism is a vital industry to Spain and has resulted in thousands of hotels of all kinds. It can be difficult to find a suitable hotel when travelling and if you cannot afford to stay in PNs it may be wisest to choose a hotel in a chain. Here are some examples.

Cadena Husa

The *Grupo Husa* was founded in 1930 and has become well established in Spain. Many of their hotels are to be found on the Mediterranean seaboard but there are some in other parts of Spain and in Kuwait, Puerto Rico, Budapest and Miami. The head office is in Barcelona. It is a card company. Tel: 91 276 71 86.

Grupo Sol

This concern has a great many hotels in the Balearics and most beachside areas. It caters mostly for the package tour trade so millions recall stays in their hotels. Although most of the hotels are in the resorts, this chain is expanding to other areas of Spain and other countries. There is good service and good food. The Sol group offer a 'Prestige' card entitling you to preferential treatment and sometimes a discount. It can be useful if you make frequent trips and it can be used in Melia hotels too. You may obtain the card from head office in Palma de Mallorca. Tel: 871 29 89 66.

Melia Hotels

This chain chiefly provides five star hotels in the main cities. The motto of this chain is 'every room in the hotel is the best'. The cuisine is good and breakfast substantial. These hotels are ideal for long business lunches. Tel: 91 241 82 00.

Novotel

This company is opening new hotels in Spain such as the Novotel Madrid which is close to the motorway leading to the airport. There are ample conference rooms and facilities for business meetings. Tel: 91 405 46 00.

TRYP Hotels

This chain is a relative newcomer to Spain using foreign capital. There is now a whole chain of four or five star hotels throughout the country. Tel: 91 315 32 46.

HOTUSA Hotels

These are increasingly seen in Spain and Spain now accounts for about half of the hotels this company holds. Tel: 93 318 45 75.

Santos Hotels

This is a company with two hotels in Madrid, one in Santander, one in Granada and another in Palma de Majorca. The hotels are specially designed for business meetings, meals, cocktails. Tel: 91 431 21 37/431 41 01. Fax: 91 577 58 35. http://www. cyber-mundi.esh/santos

Familia Hotels

This is an organisation of some seventy family hotels. It specialises in providing accommodation at reasonable prices for large families. The *familia numerosa* is still quite common in Spain and is a steady market force. Hotels are usually one to three star grade, each being run by a family with the idea of making other families feel at home. Its policy statement reads, 'a small hotel with a straightforward, friendly, family atmosphere and good sensible cooking'. This organisation is associated with 550 hotels throughout Europe including Consort Hotels in the United Kingdom, Neotel in France, HTR hotels in Austria, Landidyll in Germany, CMV Hotels in Ireland.

Familia Hotels pay great attention to good service in many ways. It provides a tourist map of Spain marking the hotels in the organisation and a booklet with the details of each hotel in the chain in six languages: English, French, German, Italian, Spanish and Catalan. The hotel Conde de Aznar in Jaca in the southern Pyrenees is recommended. Tel: 93 317 92 16.

Possible perks

If you plan to travel a great deal in Spain for business, pleasure or other reasons, it is useful to know that some of the hotel chains give cards to clients which may reduce the price of a room by 10 per cent, or in special cases, 25 per cent.

Private hotels

The advantage of staying in hotels belonging to a recognised chain is that if you have a complaint, it is more likely to be taken seriously. Foreign visitors are commenting increasingly on the worsening service in many Spanish hotels. Requesting the complaint book or form (*libro de reclamaciones u hoja*) usually has some effect. The quality of Spanish private hotels is very variable. Using one in a chain of hotels usually guarantees a degree of satisfaction.

There are good individual hotels to be found. They certainly exist but it may involve a number of unpleasant experiences before you find one. The Hotel Puerto de Pajares on the road from Asturias to Madrid is greatly recommended. It used to be a PN but is now run by the regional government at reasonable prices. It is especially attractive to groups interested in winter sports or hill walking, mountaineering and the like. Tel: 985 49 60 23.

PURSUING LEISURE ACTIVITIES

Twenty or thirty years ago it used to be necessary to explain to the majority of Spaniards (not the travelled upper class) what 'tennis' and 'golf' were. Since then there have been many successful Spanish champions in these sports and in others less well known. Spain has become a country for tennis, golf, camping, yachting, skiing, caving and many other pastimes.

The younger generation are taking a greater interest in sports these days and facilities which were scarce two decades ago are now common. Of course, all the Olympic sports have been given a tremendous boost since the Olympic Games were held in Barcelona in 1992. Patrocinadores (sponsor, patrons) are becoming widespread in Spain. Companies are not only sponsoring the Spanish Olympic teams in all kinds of sport from sailing to fencing but also cultural events.

Lovers of classical music, theatre, films and the other arts are well catered for. Any of the multitude of tourist offices will give you information on the subject. Granada has a very good classical music festival. Film festivals are staged every year at San Sebastián, Alcalá de Henares, Valladolid and other capitals. They are becoming sufficiently important to attract top stars.

You will find many suggestions in the national Press and the many foreign language publications in Spain can be very helpful. They list not only golf clubs, football and activities of general interest to Spaniards but also such activities as amateur theatricals, organised walks, art classes, cricket, bowls, Samaritans Worldwide, cottage artistry, barbecuing, polo, bridge, harriers, mountain walking, American football, animal protection societies, cross country running and so on. You might even find a train spotting club if you try hard enough!

In Spain leisure activities have given rise to important industries as much as anywhere else. Special areas of growth are golf, marinas and athletics (because of the Olympics). Even the smallest town is installing a swimming pool in the hope of encouraging a gold medallist.

Benalmádena is a perfect example of the kind of development that is taking place. Senor don Ramón Rico-Muñoz has been the mayor of Benalmádena since 1 December 1985 and one of his principal aims is to put Benalmádena on the map. It is the first resort on the Costa del Sol to have drawn up its own marketing plan. Senor Rico states to all and sundry, 'We are the first town too of our size to offer so many cultural events which include classical concerts, folk dancing and so on. We aim to promote our offer year round'. International football teams make use of this town's facilities for training as well as the locals.

Golf

The golf enthusiast will find his paradise on the Costa del Sol where there are a score of first class golf courses within a few miles of each other, many with built-in luxury housing developments. New golf courses are being projected, planned and built all the time so the selection is very wide. You should contact the Andalucian Golf Federation if you would like the latest, most detailed information. Tel: 952 22 59 90.

Some of the latest news is that a Swedish company has bought Los Naranjos Golf Club and is improving the quality of the Robert Trent Jones course and building a new clubhouse. The Swedish *Conata* group has put up 50 per cent of the capital for the Waconsa group to build a new leisure facility comprising luxury housing and a golf course designed by Severiano Ballesteros and José Luis de Bernardo. It is called *Los Arqueros* and is 10 kms from Marbella. It is thought that it will become part of the Royal Spanish Golf Federation and that it may be the venue for important tournaments.

A new course called Domayo in Galicia is being opened. It is 8 kms from Vigo and 10 kms from Pontevedra and lies beside the River Vigo, commanding exceptional views.

Veragolf is another new course designed by Seve Ballesteros. It is on the coast of Almería and its opening was planned to coincide with the 500th anniversary of Columbus' arrival in the Americas, in 1992. Again it includes a luxury housing development.

There are currently seven courses in Majorca and one each on Ibiza and Menorca, but four more are being built: Roca Viva, 71 kms from Palma de Mallorca at Capdepera, Son Termens, 12 kms from Palma de Mallorca on the Carretera de Bunyola, Santa Pinca, 18 kms from Palma de Mallorca on the Carretera de Andraix, Ibiza's new golf course, 8 kms from Elvissa on the Carretera de Sta Eulalia por Jesús.

The Balearic Golf Federation is helpful and will send information to foreign visitors and the Govern Balear will also have all the information about golf courses in the region. The Spanish themselves treat golf as something of a status symbol, making great play of using the English words, just like bottles of Scotch whisky and the pedigree dog with its British name. As Amando de Miguel writes in *Los Españoles*, 'Leisure time has less to do with Nature than might be expected. It is true that everyone says that they like the countryside, the beach, the mountains; but the favourite pastimes of the Spanish are watching television, listening to the radio and using the car'.

In spite of this definition which is mainly true, golf is a booming sport together with yachting and all concerning leisure boating.

Marinas and 'mucking about in boats'

Spain is the country with the greatest number of public holidays per year in the European Union, and these holidays alone give Spaniards plenty of time for nautical sports. Then there are normal holidays, adding an extra month or so. It is hardly surprising that marinas are mushrooming around the Spanish mainland and archipelagos. All the associated nautical sports are enjoying similar popularity. In fact, such is the popularity that even the inland province of Guadalajara sponsored a Soling class sailing boat for the Olympics and has declared itself an open port using the inland lake of Entrepeñas for the Master 470 Cup.

The market for new boats in Spain is said to be the most flourishing in the Mediterranean. On the Costa del Sol, in 1989, experts say that there were boat sales of over 8 billion pesetas. You will find a great selection of services offered, berthing and storage facilities. The Spanish Customs permits foreign registered boats to be used for six months of the year and to remain in the country for the rest of the year during which time the boat may be used for habitation. Gibraltar has two marinas which bring in 5 million per year in boat business and upkeep.

A new luxury marina and tourist development is to be built on the coast of Almeria province called Puerto Marques. It will comprise marinas, two golf courses, hotels, commercial centres and much housing. There is an international airport near Almeria now and roads are being upgraded so this area will finally be developed.

The number of marinas continues to increase in the Canary Islands too. There are now four on Tenerife, four in Gran Canaria and one each on the isles of Gomera, La Palma, Lanzarote and Fuerteventura. They are all close to airports and popular because of the year long season. Many people keep their craft on these islands since it is only 705 nautical miles from Cádiz to Tenerife and 680 nautical miles from Cádiz to Gran Canaria.

Tennis
Tennis is practised everywhere these days, helped greatly by some of the Spanish stars. Several of these, incidentally, are emigrating to Andorra to enjoy their earnings without having to pay tax. Every small town, hotel and club has its tennis court so this game may be practised year round in many parts of Spain. There are even flood-lit courts like those at the Motel Avión near Madrid's Barajas airport. Manuel Santana also owns and runs one of the best European tennis schools in Puente Romana (Málaga).

Other sports
It would require a book in itself to detail the many sports on offer in Spain. The Spanish Sports Council (*Consejo Superior de Deportes*) will supply a great deal of information about sports and the many federations which cover every activity from caving to clay pigeon shooting and rally driving. The address is: Avda Martin Fierro s/n, 28040 Madrid. Tel: 91 589 67 00. Fax: 91 589 66 14.

High quality hunting, shooting and fishing are available in Spain from salmon fishing in the northern rivers to shooting mountain goats in the Sierra de Gredos. But you must make sure that you have the right permit and know which species are pro-tected. Shooting a bear, for example, carries a £5,000 penalty and a jail sentence. Small game and fishing licences are easy to obtain.

For those with a love of the wild open spaces, all is possible in Spain with the many sierras and mountain ranges.

The mountains

Some of the mountain areas in Spain are well worth exploring on your travels around Spain like the mountains of Asturias, and moving eastwards, the Picos de Europa. The Pyrenees are a world in themselves and are now being developed as a separate region on both sides of the frontier. Jaca, St Jean Pied de Port, the Valle de Arán and Andorra are all to be recommended.

The central zones of Spain have sierras too. Gredos often has snowfalls and is surprisingly isolated, as is the Sierra de Malagón. The Sierra de Navacerrada is very popular with the Madrileños and parking can be a problem. The Sierra Nevada near Granada is also well developed.

Northern Spain

The north and north west coastal regions are also not as well known to many foreigners. There is excellent scenery, very long attractive beaches and it has long been the haunt of the wealthy Spaniard during his holidays. This included Franco. It is also ideal for those who prefer a cooler climate and rural surrounds. Galicia with its Rías Bajas and Rías Altas is an old favourite with the Spanish and well worth getting to know.

Where to eat

Eating places are best judged by the size of the clientèle. Expensive restaurants with few diners should be avoided and you should patronise those that are well frequented. The Spanish enjoy eating out so the best places will be obvious by the crowds.

10

Saving Time at Work and Play

One soon becomes acquainted with the fact that it is easy to lose time in Spain. This chapter, based on decades of experience, is a guide for those making brief trips to the country. So if your time is precious, watch out for traffic jams, and delays of all types.

TRANSPORT

The Lord Mayor of Madrid has recently inaugurated the Metro line which links Barajas airport to the centre of Madrid. This has answered a long-standing need for a rail link due to constant road blocking with traffic jams. These jams caused many travellers to arrive too late for their flights.

However, once in Barajas, there is a fully operational air bridge to Barcelona, which cuts time on that trip while the AVE line is being completed (see Chapter 9). The AVE train has been running between Seville and Madrid since 1992, and many business people save time by taking these high speed trains, as they cover the distance in two and a quarter hours with great punctuality at some 300 kmph. In fact RENFE promises that if an AVE train arrives more than five minutes late, RENFE will return the price of the ticket to the travellers – and that promise is carried out in practice.

Since priority is being given to fully extending the AVE network in the Iberian Peninsula, and to link up with the French TGV (using the same rail gauge) you should check what the latest position is especially if you do not like flying. However, travel time can also be reduced by using domestic flights, which have become increasingly common between provincial cities in France and elsewhere and cities in Spain.

Letting the *Cercanías* take the strain

These trains were known as Interurbanos, but now have changed completely. Comfortable seats are usually available (except some-times in rush hours) with good air conditioning, or heating, classical or other music, visual and audible announcements of the next station and final destination, etc. These trains can save you time in the large cities, where traffic and parking have become ever more complicated – and time consumming. They will take you right to the cities' centres and are officially encouraged in every way. In fact the President of RENFE has just announced that another 26,500 million pesetas will be invested in these *cercanías* for 46 new trains of the 447 series. Some of the *cercanías* are double decked, usually permitting room on the upper deck for paperwork, which again saves time for business people in a hurry.

Checking your appointments

If you are a business person in a hurry and have a list of interviews fixed – perhaps some time ahead – it's wise to check those appointments a day or two before. If not, the person you have to meet may be in Japan, New York or elsewhere, just taking a break, or affected by the numerous *fiestas* (public holidays in Spain).

One fact of life in Spain is that people do *not* like reading. So don't be surprised if your mail is ignored. Fax gives better results, but not 100 per cent by any means. Keeping that fact in mind could save you much time. As can taking the plane, trains, etc. after lunch, since that business lunch can become very extended. Dinner can too, even when an early start is planned next day.

SAVING TIME AT PLAY

Bene agere ac laetari (work and play well) applies as much now as in Roman times in Spain. The brief-holiday visitor should aim to use time wisely, in order to enjoy the holiday to the full.

Spanish tourist offices are generally well equipped with publications, lists, etc. of all types, to permit planning ahead and save that precious element of time. Money can also be saved by choosing the autumn and spring, when one can obtain half-price holidays through the large Spanish group of Air Europa and Halcon-Viajes, with modern aircraft, many just brought in. Being experts, they take you *rapidly* to Majorca, Menorca, etc. and many other destinations worldwide (Tel: 902 300 600).

OFFICIAL TOURIST POLICY

The official view of tourism is that 'sun and sea' holidays have grown to their maximum, and the desire now is to actively develop other types of holidays, for those visitors looking for culture, history, walking tours, adventure activities and other special interests.

The Government fully recognised tourism's importance to the Spanish economy, saying it provides 9 per cent of total national employment in Spain and 10 per cent of the GNP. It cannot be ignored – as was sometimes the practice of the previous Socialist Government. In 1996, for example, the number of foreign visitors was 61.8 million bringing \$3,499.5 million to Spain. The Secretary of State for Tourism says that tourist income increased by fully 12.5 per cent in the first eight months of 1997 to reach 2,620,000 million pesetas. This explains why official backing is so readily given to all new ventures and activities.

'The tourist industry employs nearly a million Spaniards, so that their efforts help to generate around 10 per cent of the *national* income and wealth,' says the Spanish Prime Minister, José María Aznar. 'Tourism in Spain *is fundamental to all* of us.'

Rural tourism
Rural tourism is still something of a 'new idea' in Spain, and while not up to the standard of the French *Gites* organisations, is definitely progressing, as more and more people want to 'get back to nature'. Already half a million beds are available, and regional governments are particularly interested in this 'novelty'. If you write to the region of your choice, they will gladly send details (see pages 59 and 60).

Bicycle holidays
These should be checked with your local association for road conditions as normally the highways have *no provision* for cyclists and *many die* every year in road accidents. Free motorways could be safer but great caution is advised – even if the Government says it's going to promote such holidays.

Fitur
This is the huge international tourist fair, a five-day event held at the end of January every year. Results for 1998 were: 46,000 professional visitors; 620 exhibitors; and 164 countries present.

Fitur is held in the eight giant pavilions of the IFEMA show grounds, between Madrid's centre and airport with many new hotels, congress halls, etc. alongside. The show area is 43,000 square metres, and there is parking space for some five thousand vehicles. Even for the 'layman' it makes an interesting visit, and helps holiday planning.

Naturism

Costa Natura is a naturist village on the Costa del Sol, west of Málaga. Nearby are seveal naturist beaches which are quite famous and popular in Andalucia. Vera beach is over a mile long with fine yellow sand, and peaceful surroundings. Alongside is the Hotel Vera Playa, Spain's unique naturist hotel, which provides very pleasant surroundings 'in the raw'. Its swimming pool is ideal for the family holiday with ample space to enjoy life without clothes. Every facility is offered. The large patio interior is well furnished and is used for evening entertainments. The hotel is very popular, especially with Brits, although many other languages are heard there too. (Tel: 950 46 74 13. Fax: 950 46 74 75).

Naturism is officially permitted on numerous beaches as shown in the list below. ANA (Asociacion Naturista de Andalucia) gives full information about those in Andalucia (address: PO Box 301, Almeria). Other associations exist around the coastal areas (see list).

Madrid's naturists complain that they have little freedom of movement, apart from small areas in the swimming pools at El Pilar, and La Elipa (without pool usage). However, the deputies in the IU Party are pressing for greater facilities for naturists in the Madrid region, to include pool usage, sections of parks and natural reserves and the like. This has been passed to be considered for legislation and progress is promised, backed by deputies led by Luis Miguel Sánchez Seseña, of the IU Party, who points out that no advance has been made since 1 August 1986, and it is time 'to ask for more'!

Festivals

Festivals are also being encourage by the Administration. Film festival events are held all over the country, even in small cities, and attract the stars. The same applies to classical music in Granada, Cuenca, Vitoria and the Canary Isles. Again, they bring in the top names with excellent results.

NATURIST ASSOCIATIONS

CCN. Club Català Naturisme, Hotel d'Entitats, c/Concili de Trento 313, Bústia 3.110, 08021 Barcelona. Tel: 93 278 02 94. Fax: 93 278 01 74.

ADN. Asociación para el Desarrollo Naturista de la Comunidad de Madrid, Apartado 50.370. 28080 Madrid.

ANAR. Asociación Naturista Aragonesa, Apartado 474, 50080 Zaragoza.

ANVA. Asociación Naturista Valenciana, Apartat 694, 46080 València.

ANE. As. Naturista de Euskadi, Apartado 861, 48080 Bilbo.

NATURIST BEACHES

Andalucía
Almería
Cabo de Gata
Mojácar, en Torre del Peñón
Roquetas de Mar, Playa Cerrilios
Vera, junto Hotel Vera Playa

Cádiz
Barbate, Los Caños de Meca
Chipiona

Granada
Almuñécar, Playa de la Herradura

Huelva
Playa de la Antilla

Málaga
Estepona, Costa Natura
Marbella, Las Dunas-Carib Playa

Asturias
Llanes, playe de Torimbia
Gijón, playas de Peñarrubia y Serin

Cantabria
Langre, playa de las Arenas
Bahía de Somo (zona central)

Catalunya
Barcelona
Arenys de Mar, Cala Musclera (Restaurante Hispania)
Badalona, playa de la Mora (fábrica Cros)
Calella, calas del faro y Pere
Sant Pol de Mar, playa del Refugi (km 662.4 de la N-2)
Stiges, cala de l'Home Mort
Viladecans

Girona
Begur, playas Illa Roja y de Pals
Cadaqués, playa del cabo de Creus
Calella de Palafrugell, cala Estreta (cámping Benelux)
Castelló d'Empúries, bahía de Roses (cámping La Laguna)
Lloret de Mar, cala Boadella (hotel Fanals)
Sant Pere Pescador, desembocadura de Fluvià
Tossa de Mar, calas Corrullada y Vallpresona

Tarragona
Altafulla, cala de la Mora
L'Hospitalet de l'enfant, cala Justell y playa del Torn
Sant Jaume d'Enveja, playa del Trabucador

Euskadi (Basque Country)
Bizkaia
Larrabasterra, playa de Túnel Boca

Gipuzkoo
Donostia, Playa de Tximist arri, Monte Igeldo
Zarautz, Playa final sector Este

Galicia
A Coruña
A Corña, playa de Barrañán y playa de Traba
Camariñas, Arenas Blancas/Faro Vilana
El Ferrol, playa Lume Boo y playa de Cobas en Cabo Prior
Muros, playa de Lariño y Louro

Pontevedra
Cangas, playa de Vilariño
Pontevedra, playa de Melille (isla de Ons)
Sanxenxo, playa de Bascuas
Vigo, playa de los Almanes (en las Islas Cies)
Cangas de Morrazo, playa de la Barra

Murcia
Cala Reona, entre el cabo de Palos y Cartagena
Cala Bolnuevo (sur de Mazarrón)

Pais Valencià
Alacante
Cala de los Judos (cabo de las Huertas, cafetería El Tobo) y playa
de El Saladar (carretera a Cartagena)
L'Alfàs de Pi (carretera de Albir al faro)
Altea, cala Olla al sur del Cabo Els Mascarats
Dènia, cala de Les Rotes
Elx, playa del Carabassi (hotel Los Arenales del Sol)
Guardamar del Segura, playa de els Tosals, La Vila Joiosa, cala
Racó del Conill
Xàbia, cala de Ambolo

Castelló
Playa entre Orpesa y Ribera de Cabanes, sector central

València
Playa de El Saler (sector al norte del parador nacional)

Motoring
Touring by car is popular with visitors to Spain, because of the wide variety of scenery and the well-conserved historical buildings in most parts. Now that petrol stations are more numerous, there is little danger of running out of fuel as in yesteryear. But if you want or need to save time, keep to motorways as off-beat roads can be very time-consuming.

FAREWELL OR *HASTA LA VISTA*

So there you have some of the multitude of offers open to visitors to Spain. And the Government is definitely promoting new forms of tourism, so more are expected. If your visit is brief – oh! so brief – we hope next time it will be longer. It could even last a lifetime – as has happened to many of us. Hasta la vista!

Useful Addresses

EMBASSIES AND CONSULATES

The British Consulate, Edificio Cataluña PO Box 2020, 5 Luis Morote 6-3, Puerto de la Luz, 35007 Las Palmas, Canary Islands. Tel: 928 26 25 08. Fax: 928 267774.

The British Consulate, Plaza Nueva 8-Dpdo, 41001 Seville. Tel: 95 422 88 75. Fax: 95 421 0323.

The British Consulate-General, Avda de la Fuerzas, Armadas 11, Algeciras. Tel: 95 666 16 00.

The British Consulate-General, Avda Diagonal 477-13°, 08036 Barcelona. Tel: 93 419 90 44. Fax: 93 405 24 11.

The British Consulate-General, Alameda de Urquijo 2-8, 48008 Bilbao. Tel: 94 415 76 00. Fax: 94 416 76 32.

The British Consulate. Plaza Calvo Sotelo 1/2, 03001, Alicante. Tel: 965 21 60 22/21 61 90. Fax: 965 14 05 28.

The British Vice-Consulate, Avda de Isidoro Macabith 45, 07800, Ibiza. Tel: 971 30 18 18/30 38 16. Fax: 971 30 19 72.

The British Consulate, Edificio Duquesa, Duquesa de Parcent 8-1, 29001 Málaga. Tel: 95 221 75 71. Fax: 95 221130.

HM Consul, Plaza Mayor 3D, 07002 Palma de Mallorca. Tel: 971 71 24 45. Fax: 971 71 75 20.

Hon. British Consulate, Paseo de Pereda 27, 39004 Santander. Tel: 942 22 00 00. Fax: 942 22 29 41.

The British Consulate-General, Santian 4, Tarragona. Tel: 97 720 12 46.

The British Consulate, Plaza Weyler 8-1, 38003 Santa Cruz de Tenerife. Tel: 922 28 68 63. Fax: 922 28 99 03.

Hon. British Consulate, Prat de la Creu 22 bl D Alt 2, Andorra la Vella, Andorra. Tel: 376 86 77 31. Fax: 376 86 77 31.

The British Consulate, Plaza Compostela 23-6, 36201 Vigo. Tel: 986 43 71 33. Fax: 986 43 71 33.

The British Embassy, calle de Fernando el Santo 16, 28010 Madrid. Tel: 419 02 00, 419 02 12, telex: 27656 a/b 27656 INGLA E, fax: 419-0423.

The Spanish Consulate-General, 63 North Castle Street, Edinburgh EH2 3LJ. Tel: 0131 220 1843.

The Spanish Consulate-General, 70 Spring Gardens, Manchester M2 2BQ. Tel: (0161) 236 1233.

The Spanish Consulate-General, 20 Draycott Place SW3 2RZ. Tel: (0207) 589 8989.

The Spanish Embassy, 16th Floor, Portland House, Stag Place, London SW1E 5SE. Tel: (0207) 235 5555.

TRAVEL

Contacts in Britain

British Airways Travel Division, PO Box 115, West London Air Terminal, Cromwell Road, London SW7 4ED. Tel: (0207) 370 4255.

British Rail Continental Enquiries. Tel: (0208) 834 2345.

Brittany Ferries, Millbay Docks, Plymouth PL1 3EW. Tel: (01752) 221321. Tel: (01752) 269926 for brochures.

Institute of Spain, 102 Eaton Square SW1. Tel: (0207) 235 1485.

Spanish Airlines (IBERIA), Venture House, 29 Glass House St, London W1R 5RG.

Spanish Aviation Services, 57B Lupus Street SW1. Tel: (0207) 821 5801.

Spanish National Tourist Office, 57-58 St James St, London SW1. Tel: (0207) 499 0901.

Trásmediterraneo, Melia Travel, 12 Dover St, London W1. Tel: (0207) 409 1884.

Contacts in Spain

Ayuda en Carretera (help on the road). Tel: 91 742 12 13.

Ayuntamientos (town halls).

British Airways, Serrano 60-5, 28001 Madrid.

Central de Reservas e Información Internacional, Instituto de la Juventud, (youth hostels) calle José Ortega y Gasset 71, 28006 Madrid. Tel: 91 401 13 00.

Consejeros de Turismo (Ministers of Tourism, one in each region).

Delegación Española de la Federación Internacional de Camping, Edificio España (grupo 4° 11), 28013 Madrid. Tel: 91 542 10 89. (Camping, discount card and hitchhiking card.)

Flebasa Lines, Estación Maritima, Denia (Alicante). Tel: 96 578 40 11. Fax: 96 57 87 606/605. (Connections between Denia and Ibiza, Altea and Formentera.)

Iberrail SA, calle Capitán Haya 55, 28020 Madrid. El Andalus.

Información IBERIA. Tel: 91 411 25 45.

Información RENFE (Spanish Railways), Tel: 91 411 25 45. Special excursions. Tel: 91 733 62 00. El Transcantábrico: 91 253 76 56.

Ministerio de Cultura, Instituto de la Juventud, José Ortega y Gasset 71, 28006 Madrid. Tel: 91 401 13 00. (Youth or student travel.)

Real Automóvil Club de España (RACE), José Abascal 10, 28003 Madrid. (The equivalent of the AA.)

Secretaria General de Turismo MTTC, calle María de Molina 50, 28006 Madrid. Tel: 91 411 40 14/411 60 11. Telex: 23284. (General information.)

TIVE, Fernando el Católico 88, 28015 Madrid. Tel: 91 232 1300 (Student travel.)

ACCOMMODATION

Asociación Nacional de Estaciones Termales (ANET), calle Martin de los Heros 23-4° dcha B, 28008 Madrid. Tel: 91 542 97 75. Fax: 542 98 24. (National association of spas.)

Cadena Husa, Rambla Cataluna 20, 08007 Barcelona. Tel: 93 318 13 86, 317 27 00. HUSA Central Booking Office, Paseo de la Castellana 12-6°, 28046 Madrid. Tel: 91 276 71 86, 275 12 00. Telex: 54134. (Chain of hotels.)

Familia Hotels, Central de Reservas, calla Canuda 20, 08002 Barcelona (Catalunya). Tel: 93 317 92 16. Telex: 59376. Fax: 93 317 92 16.

Federación Española de Montana, calle Alberto Aguilera 3, 28015 Madrid. Tel: 91 445 13 82. (Mountain refuges.)

Hotusa, calle Balmes 12 pral 1, 08007 Barcelona. Tel: 93 318 45 75. Telex: 98201. Fax: 93 318 73 38.

Hotel Puerto de Pajares, Principado de Asturias. PO Box 1348, 33080 Oviedo. Tel: 985 49 60 23. Telex: 84003.

Institute of Foreign Property Owners, calle Conde de Altea 33, 03550 Altea (Alicante). Tel: 96 584 23 12.

Melia Hotels, calle Princesa 27, 28008 Madrid. Tel: 91 541 82 00, 541 84 00. Fax: 91 541 19 88. Telex: 22537 METEL-E.

Freephone: 900 14 44 44. Also Brushfield Street, London E1. Tel: (0207) 375 2121. Fax: (0207) 375 0377.

Novotel, calle Albacete 1, 28037 Madrid. Tel: 91 405 46 00. Telex: 41862 NOVMD. Fax: 91 404 11 05.

Paradores Nacionales, calle Velasquez 18, 28001 Madrid, PO Box 50043, 28082 Madrid. Tels: 91 435 97 00, 435 97 44, 435 98 14. Fax: 91 435 99 44. (Main Reservations.) Also, United Kingdom: Keytel International, 402 Edgware Road, London W2 1ED. Tel: (0207) 402 8182. Telex: 21780. Also, United States: US Marketing Ahead Inc, 433 Fifth Avenue, New York NY10016. Tel: 686 9213. Telex: 22 00 26.

Santos Hoteles, calle Juan Bravo 8, Madrid. Tel: 91 431 21 37, 431 18 97. Telex: 41980. Fax: 91 577 58 35.

Sol Group, Central de Reservas, Edificio Grupo Sol, calle Gremio Toneleros 42, Poligono San Castello, 07009 Palma de Mallorca. Tel: 871 29 89 66, 25 20 52, 29 96 540. Telex: 68539.

Spanish Property Consultants (Estate Agents), 6 Fernhead Road, London NW4. Tel: (0208) 968 7619.

Spanish Property Owners Association, 1109 Finchley Road, London NW11. Tel/Fax: (0208) 209 1951.

Spanish Property Services, Sunset Lodge, Cedars Close, London NW4. Tel: (0208) 203 4140.

Spanish Sun Properties Ltd, 7 The Quadrant, Hoylake, Merseyside. Tel: (0207) 628 2484.

TRYP hotels, calle Mauricio Legendre 16, 28046 Madrid. Tel: 91 315 32 46. Telex: 42920 TRYCP E.

CULTURAL, EDUCATIONAL AND SOCIAL

Andalusian Sailing Federation. Tel: 952 87 03 03.

Andalusian Golf Federation. Tel: 952 22 59 90.

Andalusian Tennis Federation. Tel: 952 26 38 39.

Balearic Golf Federation, Avda Rey Jaime III-17 dcha 16, 07012 Palma de Mallorca. Tel: 971 72 27 53.

Ciudad Universitaria s/n, 28040 Madrid. Tel: 91 549 77 00. (Information about university education.)

Central Bureau for Educational Visits and Exchanges, Seymour Mews House, Seymour Mews, London W1H 9PE. Tel: (0207) 486 5101.

Consejo Superior de Deportes, Avda Martin Fierro s/n, 28003 Madrid. Tel: 91 449 73 00, 243 36 06. (Sports information.)

Federación Española de Actividades Subacuáticos, calle Santaló 15-2°. Barcelona. (Underwater sports.)

Federación Española de Golf, calle Capitán Haya 9, 28020 Madrid. Tel: 91 455 26 82, 445 87 15, 455 13 93. (Golf.)

Federación Española de Vela, calle Juan Vigón 23, Madrid. Tel: 91 533 53 05, 233 84 08. (Sailing.)

Govern Balear, Consellería de Turismo, calle Montenegro 5, 07012 Palma de Mallorca. Tel: 971 71 20 22. Telex: 69346 CTIB E.

Ministerio de Culturo (Servicio de Publicaciones), calle Fernando el Católico 77, 28015 Madrid. Tel: 91 544 56 18. (Information.)

Ministerio de Educación y Ciencias (MEC), Alcalá 34, 28014 Madrid. Tel: 91 532 13 00. (Ministry of Education.)

Servicio de Información del MEC, Alcalá 36, 28014 Madrid. Tel: 91 521 48 06, 521 45 30, 532 13 00. (Information on education.)

Relaciones Culturales Internacionales, Ferraz 82 2°, 28008 Madrid. Tel: 91 479 63 03.

Spanish Club, 5, Cavendish Square, London W1. Tel: (0207) 580 2750.

Spanish Embassy Education Office, 20 Peel Street, London W8 7PD. Tel: (0207) 727 2462.

BUSINESS CONTACTS

Business contacts in Britain

British Council, 10 Spring Gardens, London SW1. Tel: (0207) 930 8466.

Department of Trade and Industry Overseas Trade Division (Spain Desk), 1 Victoria St, London SW1H 0ET. Tel: (0207) 215 4284 (Capital goods), 215 5624 (Consumer goods).

Inland Revenue Claims Branch, Foreign Division, Merton Rd, Bootle L69 9BL.

Internal European Policy Division, Department of Trade and Industry, Room 418, 1 Victoria St, London SW1X 0ET. Tel: (0207) 215 5354. (Certificates of Professional Equivalence.)

Spanish Agencies, Mfrs Agent, 160 Castle Hill, Reading. Tel: (01734) 509339.

Spanish Citrus Management Committee, 23 Manchester Square, London W1. Tel: (0207) 486 3476.

The Spanish Embassy (Commercial Office), 22 Manchester Square W1. Tel: (0207) 486 0101.

Spanish Institute (Instituto de España), 102 Eaton Square, London SW1. Tels: (0207) 235 1484, 235 1485.
Spanish Promotion Centre, 23 Manchester Square, London W1. Tel: (0207) 935 6140.

Business contacts in Spain

British Chamber of Commerce in Spain, Plaza Santa Barbara 10, 28010 Madrid. Tel: 91 308 3081/4.
British Council, Plaza Santa Barbara 10, 28010 Madrid. Tel: 91 319 1250.
British Institute, Almagro 5, 28003 Madrid. Tel: 91 319 12 50.
Communications General Directorate, calle Ayalá 5, 28001 Madrid. Tel: 91 448 70 00. Fax: 91 435 55 23.
General Directorate of Customs, calle Guzmán el Bueno 137, 28003 Madrid. Tel: 91 553 02 00. Fax: 91 533 52 42.
General Directorate of Foreign Commerce, Paseo de la Castellana 162, 28046 Madrid. Tel: 91 458 00 16. Fax: 91 559 44 66.
General Directorate of Foreign Transactions, Paseo de la Castellana 162, 28046 Madrid. Tel: 91 559 57 01. Fax: 91 571 16 59.
Income Tax Revenue Bureau, calle Guzmán el Bueno 139, 28020 Madrid. Tel: 91 550 39 00. Fax: 91 550 51 00.
Industrial Property Registry, calle Panamá 1, 28036 Madrid. Tel: 91 458 22 00.
Instituto Nacional de la Seguridad Social Subdirección General de Relaciones Internacionales, Padre Damien 4, Madrid 16. (The Spanish equivalent of the DSS.)
Ministry of Agriculture, Paseo Infanta Isabel 1, 28014 Madrid. Tel: 91 347 50 00.
Ministry of Economy and Finance, calle Alcalá 9, 28014 Madrid. Tel: 91 468 20 00. Telex: 27811.
Ministry of External Affairs, Plaza de la Provincia 1, 28012 Madrid. Tel: 91 566 48 00. Fax: 91 566 70 76.
Ministry of Industry and Energy, Paseo de la Castellana 160, 28046 Madrid. Tel: 91 458 80 10. Fax: 91 457 80 66.
Ministry of Labour and Social Security, calle Augustín de Bethancourt 4, 28003 Madrid. Tel: 91 553 60 00. Fax: 91 533 29 96.
Spanish Employers' Organisation, calle Diego de León 50, 28006 Madrid. Tel: 91 563 96 41. Fax: 91 562 80 23.

BRITISH BANKS IN SPAIN

Banco NatWest March SA, Miguel Angel 23, 28010 Madrid. Tel 91 419 11 12.

Barclays Bank, Madrid Main Branch, Plaza de Colón 1, 28046, Madrid. Tel: 91 410 2800, 319 9014.

Grindlays Bank, Paseo de la Castilla, 28046 Madrid.

Lloyds Bank International plc, calle Serrano 90, 28006 Madrid. Postal address: Apartado Postal 64, 28080 Madrid. Tel: 91 520 99 00, 901 10 90 00.

Midland Bank, 1st Floor Edificio Beatriz, 28006 Madrid. PO Box 2472, calle José Ortega y Gasset 29, Madrid. (Now HSBC)

LEGAL CONTACTS

Enquiries

The Legal Department, Spanish Embassy, 24 Belgrave Square, London SW1X 8QA. (Background information on buying property in Spain, Spanish succession law and setting up business in Spain.)

General: lawyers

Amhurst Brown Colombotti, 2 Duke St, St James's, London SW1Y 6BJ. Tel: (0207) 930 2366. Telex: 261857. Fax (0207) 930 2250. (Has agents throughout Spain.)

Andrews McQueen, 1613 Wimborne Road, Kinson, Bournemouth, Dorset BH11 9AP. Tel: (01202) 582582. Fax: (01202) 576262. (English solicitors dealing with Spanish law.)

T T Bennett, Bennett and Co, Bridge House, 2 Heyes Lane, Alderley Edge, Cheshire SK9 7JY. Tel: (01625) 586937. Telex: 585362. Fax: (01625) 6655566. (English solicitors dealing with property and other work in Spain.)

Anthony Bertin and Associates, Tontine House, Tontine St, Folkstone, Kent CT20 1UB. Tel: (01303) 46000. Telex: 965891 TONLAW. (English solicitors with associated offices in Madrid, Málaga and Marbella.)

Brooke North and Goodwin, Yorkshire House, East Parade, Leeds LS1 5SD. Tel: (0113) 832100. Fax: (0113) 833999. (English solicitors and Notaries Public dealing with property and commercial work in Spain and internationally.)

Davis Arnold Cooper, 12 Bridewell Place, London EC4 6AD. Tel: (0207) 353 6555. Fax: (0207) 936 2020. Associates: Abogados Ruiz Gallardon de Muniz.

De Beristain Humphrey, Theodore Goddard, 16 St Martins Le Grand, London EC1A 4EJ. Tel: (0207) 606 8855. Telex: 884678. Fax: (0207) 606 4390. (Associated office in Madrid.)

De Pinna Scorers and John Venn, 3 Albemarle St, London W1X 3HF. Tel: (0207) 409 3188. Telex: 895 1242. Fax: (0207) 491 2302. (English Notaries Public; the firm has contact with Spanish lawyers.)

Glaisyers, Alpha Tower, Suffolk St, Queensway, Birmingham B1 1TR. Tel: (0121) 632 5881. Telex: 338610. (Associated offices in various parts of Spain including the Balearics, Barcelona, Marbella, Tenerife, Valencia.)

John Howell and Co, 8 Bolton St, Piccadilly, London W1Y 8AU. Tel: (0207) 495 2361. Fax: (0207) 629 4460. (Services include conveyancing and other land related work. Associated offices covering most parts of Spain including the Balearic and Canary Islands.)

M J Soul, Michael Soul and Associates, 20 Essex St, London WC2R 3AL. Tel: (0207) 242 0848, 242 0836, 242 8400. Telex: 296342 SOULAW G. Fax: (0207) 240 2278. (Solicitor of the Supreme Court of England and Wales. Associated with offices in Madrid, Barcelona, Marbella, Palma de Mallorca and Málaga.)

D W Julian and Co, 14 Kennington Rd, London SE1 7BL. Tel: (0207) 928 8021. Telex: 261951 JULIAN G. Fax: (0207) 633 9487. (English Notaries Public who have contacts with Spanish lawyers in Madrid, Barcelona, Valencia, Alicante and Málaga.)

M E Thomas, Staffurth and Bray, York Road Chambers, Bognor Regis, West Sussex PO21 1LT. Tel: (01243) 864001. Fax: (01243) 86078. (Advises on Spanish property.)

Hugh James Jones and Jenkins, Arlbee House, Greyfriars Rd, Cardiff CF1 4BQ. Tel: (02920) 224871. Fax: (02920) 388222. (Associates in Spain.)

Michael Horton and Co, 692 Warwick Rd, Solihull, West Midlands B91 3DX. Tel: (0121) 704 2186. English solicitors. Spanish speaking lawyer provides advice on property purchase and notarial services. Costa Brava.

D B Jones, Wallers, Pearl Assurance House, 7 New Bridge St, Newcastle upon Tyne NE1 8BJ. (Deals with exporting advice and setting up businesses in Spain.)

Colin Whyman, Champion Miller and Honey, 151 High St, Tenterden, Kent TN30 6JT.

Wilde Sapte, Queensbridge House, 60 Upper Thames St, London EC4V 3BD. Tel: (0207) 236 3050. Fax: (0207) 236 9624.

Some Spanish lawyers practising in the United Kingdom

L R Barrero, Amhurst Brown Colombotti, 2 Duke St, St James's, London SW1Y 6BJ. Tel: (0207) 930 2366. Fax: (0207) 930 2250. (Member of the Madrid Bar, also admitted as Solicitor of the Supreme Court of England and Wales. Preferred fields of practice: property, probate, commercial, general advice on Spanish law.)

Canovas Sierra Torres and Co, 11 Yeoman House, The Pavement, Ealing, London W5 4NG. Tel: (0208) 566 2567. Fax: (0208) 566 1903.

Francisco Cantos, Stephenson Harwood, 1 St Paul's Churchyard, London EC1M 8SH. Tel: (0207) 329 4422. (Member of the Madrid Bar Association.)

J B de Abando, 2 Wellington Square, London SW3. Tel: (0207) 730 7384. Telex: 299778. (Member of the Bilbao Bar. Preferred fields of practice: general practice including conveyancing and commercial law.)

Antonio de Fortuny, 16 Rex Place, London W1Y 5PP. Tel: (0207) 499 2338. (Preferred fields of practice: general practice including conveyancing and commercial law.)

Jose Maria de Lorenzo, 8/12 New Bridge St, London EC4V 6AL. Tel: (0207) 583 6995. (Member of the Barcelona Bar. Preferred fields of practice: Personal injuries, property law, probate, matrimonial, commercial law and general advice.)

Diaz-Bastien and Truan, 111 Park St, London W1Y 3FB. Tel: (0207) 409 2018. Fax: (0207) 629 2902. (Paloma Peman Domecq, Member of the Málaga Bar.)

Antonio Irastorza, Boodle Hatfield, 43 Brook St, London W1Y 2BL. Tel: (0207) 629 7411. Telex: 261414. Fax: (0207) 629 2621. (Member of the Madrid Bar. Also admitted as a solicitor of the Supreme Court of England and Wales.)

José Medio and Co, 14 Dover St, London W1X 3PH. Tel: (0207) 409 2355. Telex: 21551 BROKMI G. (Mr Medio: Member of the Oviedo Bar, Mr Prado: Member of the Madrid Bar, Mr Quadra: Member of the Málaga Bar. Preferred fields of practice: general practice including property law, company law, foreign investment in Spain, probate, preparation of Spanish legal documents and taxation law.)

Elena Perez Carillo, Bertin Ware and Associates, Tontine House, Tontine St, Folkestone, Kent CT20 1UB. Tel: (01303) 46000.

E Picanol, Bufete Cuatrecasas, 41 Dover St, London W1X 3RB. Tel: (0207) 499 3186. Telex: 261576 BERGUL. (Member of the Barcelona Bar. General practice (by appointment only).)

Prado, Asua and Co, 9 Young St, Kensington, London W8 5EH. Tel: (0207) 376 0517. (Julio Prado LL M, Luis de Asua, Lourdes Portela, Members of the Madrid Bar Association.)

Fernando Scornik, 3rd Floor, 32 St James's St, London SW1A 1HD. Tel: (0207) 839 1581. Telex: 263593 SELECT-G. (Member of the Las Palmas Bar. Practises in the Canary Islands and visits London by appointment only.)

Jan Malinoski, De Anna Scories and John Venn (Notaries Public), 3 Albermarle St, London W1X 3HF. Tel: (0207) 409 3188. Fax: (0207) 491 7302. (Member of the Barcelona Bar.)

Some English lawyers who deal with Spanish law

John Reay-Smith, Al Huerta de Los Naranjos, Peunte Mayorga, Cádiz.

Agusten Gill de Antunano, Monte Esquinza 26 5 Dcha, 28010 Madrid. Tel: 91 419 54 31, 419 26 31. Telex: 45441. London office: Stoneham Langton and Passmore, 8 Bolton St, Piccadilly, London W1Y 8AU. Tel: (0207) 499 8000. Telex: 21640.

Baker and McKenzie, Pinar 18, 28006 Madrid. Tel: 91 411 30 62. Fax: 91 562 24 25. London office: Aldwych House, Aldwych, London WC2B 4JP. Tel: (0207) 242 6531. Fax: (0207) 831 8611.

Brebner and Co, Paseo de la Castellana no 143/2V, 28016 Madrid. Tel: 91 270 27 44, 270 27 81. London office: 107 Cheapside, London EC2V 6DT. Tel: (0207) 600 0885. Telex: 895 0075 DESK G. Fax: (0207) 726 2816.

Despatcho Juridico, Castello 128, 28006 Madrid. Tel: 91 563 10 86. Telex: 45060. Fax: 91 563 99 76. Mr O C Vero, an English solicitor admitted to the Spanish Bar. London office: Clifford Chance, Blackfriars House, 19 New Bridge St, London EC4V 6BY. Tel: (0207) 353 0211. Telex: 887847.

A V B Grant, Celsa de la Pena Abogados, Almagro 2, 28010 Madrid. Tels: 91 410 17 64, 410 35 09, 410 02 85. Telex: 43278 PLEA E. Fax: 91 410 6586. English solicitor working for a firm of Spanish lawyers.

Alexander Pitts, Abogados, Goya 63, 28001 Madrid. Tel: 91 576 52 95. Telex: 45581. Fax: 91 575 55 42. (English barrister, also admitted to Spanish Bar.)

Frank Porral, Marques del Riscal 11-Dpdo, 28010 Madrid. Tel: 91 419 75 75, 419 75 69. Telex: 46176 GFCC-E. (English barrister, also admitted to Spanish Bar.)

R M Smeaton, Gomez-Acebo y Pombo, Castellana 164, Madrid 28046. Tel: 91 250 72 00. Telex: 23429. (English solicitor working for a firm of Spanish lawyers.)

Stephenson Harwood, Marques del Riscal 11 5, 28010 Madrid. Tel: 91 410 09 66. Telex: 22469. Fax: Groups 2 and 3, 91 410 2882. London office: Saddlers' Hall, Gutter Lane, Cheapside, London EC2V 6BS. Tel: (0207) 606 7733. Telex: 886789 LIMATO G. Fax: Groups 2 and 3, (0207) 606 0822.

Edward Wiltshire, Lagasca 106 3-Drcha, 28006 Madrid. Tel: 91 575 03 24/575 75 27. Telex: 46521. Fax: 91 435 40 89. (English solicitor.)

Peter Herbert Langdon, Linda Vista Baja, calle las Adelfas 216, San Pedro de Alcántara, Málaga.

Ashton Hill Bond, Ricardo Soriena 36 ED, Marias III 2° 208, 29600 Marbella, Málaga. Tel: 91 177 82 90. (Associated offices in Nottingham and London.)

V E Callaghan, Apartado 346, Puerto de la Cruz, Tenerife, Canaries. English barrister.

Some lawyers in Madrid (who can correspond in English)

Sr D Ignacio Gómez-Acebo & Duque de Estrado, Gómez Acebo y Pombo, Castellana 164, 2a entreplanta, 28046 Madrid. Tel: 91 582 91 00. Fax: 91 3453679/5829114. Telex: 48792 APO E/Telex: 23429 GAPOE.

Asesora Jurídica Baker & McKenzie, Pinar 18, 28006 Madrid. Tel: 91 411 30 62. Fax: 91 562 24 25.

Sr D Gustova López-Muñoz y Larraz, Calle Ferraz 49–70 dcha, 28008 Madrid. Tel: 91 542 58 65. Fax: 91 548 32 80.

Sr R Leal Perez Olague, Sor Angela de la Cruz 7–1c, 28020 Madrid. Tel: 91 597 17 57. Fax: 91 597 31 23.

Sr Javier Barrilero Yárnoz, Jusfinder, c/ Goya 48, bajo dcha, 28001 Madrid. Tel: 91 431 37 75-02. Fax: 91 575 61 64.

Fernando Scornik Gerstein, Jaime Valera y Martos, c/ Alberto Alcocer 7, 3° izda, 28036 Madrid. Tel: 91 350 72 62. Fax: 91 350 73 06.

Mr Edward Wiltshire, Lagasca 106 3-Drcha, 28006 Madrid. Tel: 91 575 03 24/575 75 27. Telex: 46521. Fax: 4354089.

D Luis Carlos Rodrigo, Bufete L C Rodrigo, c/ Velazquez 75, 28006 Madrid. Tel: 91 435 54 12. Fax: 91 576 67 16.

Celsa de la Peña, Almagro 2–3 izda, 28010 Madrid. Tel: 91 310 02 85/35 09. Fax: 91 310 00 88.

Sebastian E Muñoz Muñoz, J Hurtado de Mendoza 9, 28036 Madrid. Tel: 91 350 12 56/882 81 45. Fax: 91 345 81 05.

Balms Abogados (lawyers), Sr Juan Luis Balsameda, y Díez de Ahumada, c/ Rodríguez San Pedro 2, despacho 711, 28015 Madrid. Tel: 91 594 26 49. Fax: 91 593 41 62.

Julia Sanchez Martin, c/ Mayor 46–48, 4th floor, 28013 Madrid. Tel: 91 547 52 02. Fax: 91 547 52 01.

English solicitors in Gibraltar (dealing with Spanish law)

Brooke-North and Goodwin, 2 Irish Place, Gibraltar. Tel: 350 70545. Leeds Office: Yorkshire House, East Parade, Leeds LS1 5SD. Tel: (0113) 832100.

Glaisyers, 3 Parliament Lane, Gibraltar. Birmingham Office: 10 Rochester Court, Printing House Street, Birmingham B4 6DH.

SOME BRITISH SCHOOLS IN THE MADRID AREA

(Members of the NABSS, National Association of British Schools in Spain, except as stated).

The British Council School (Nursery–Year 13), c/ Solano 3–7, Prado de Somosaguas, 28223 Madrid. Tel: 91 337 36 12.

Kings College (Nursery–Year 13), Paseo de los Andes s/n, Soto de Viñuelas, 28761 Madrid. Tel: 91 803 48 00.

Runnymede College (Nursery–Year 13), Camino Ancho 87, La Moraleja, 28109 Alcobendas. Tel: 91 650 83 02/650 85 02.

St Ann's School (Senior School), Pinar 22, 28006 Madrid. Tel: 91 563 51 82. (Junior School) Tormes 5, 28002 Madrid. (Kindergarten) Jarama 9, 28002 Madrid. Tel: 91 563 58 30.

Hastings School (Secondary), Paseo de la Habana 204, 28036 Madrid. Tel: 91 359 99 13. Hastings Primary School, Avda Alfonso XIII, 117–119, 28016 Madrid. Tel: 91 359 31 22.

International School of Madrid (2–18 years), Rosa Jardon 3, 28016 Madrid. Tel: 91 359 21 21.

Hill House Montessori School (Years 7–9), c/ Azulinas 8, 28036 Madrid. Tel: 91 358 33 68.

Numont School (Nursery and primary, non-Spanish pupils only), Calle Parma 16, 28043 Madrid. Tel: 91 300 24 31 (general enquiries).

The English Montessori School (Nursery–11 years), Avda de la Salle s/n, 28023 Aravaca (Madrid). Triana 65 and Eduardo Vela 10. Tel: 91 357 26 67/8 or 357 21 26/7.

Kensington School (Nursery–Year 9), Avda de Bularas 2, Pozuelo de Alarcón, 28223 Madrid. Tel: 91 715 47 97/715 46 99.

St Michael's School (Nursery), Avda de la Victoria 96, 28023 Madrid. Tel: 91 307 71 74.

International College, Spain, Calle Vereda Norte 3, La Moraleja (Madrid). Tel: 91 650 23 98/99. Fax: 91 650 10 35.

Full lists for schools in Spain can be obtained from the British Council or the NABSS at the following addresses:

NABSS, Avda Cuidad de Barcelona 110, esc 3, 5D, 28007 Madrid. Tel: 91 552 05 16.

British Council, Po Gral. Martinez Campos 31, 28010 Madrid. Tel: 91 337 35 00.

MISCELLANEOUS

BUPA, 102 Queens Road Brighton BN1 3XT. In Spain: Apartado de Correos 16, 29120 Alhaurin el Grande (Málaga). Tel: 952 49 11 15.

Danmark AS International Health Insurance, Edificio el Ancla 603, 29640 Fuengirola (Málaga). Tel: 952 47 12 04. Fax: 952 47 12 08.

Department of Social Security, Overseas Branch, Central Office, Long Benton, Newcastle upon Tyne, NE98 1YX. Tel: (0191) 213 50 00.

Employment Services, Overseas Placing Unit (OPS 5), Moorfoot, Sheffield S1 4PQ.

Exeter Hospital Aid Society, 5 Palace Gate Exeter, Devon EX1 1UE.

The Federation of Recruitment and Employment Services Ltd, 36-38 Mortimer St, London W1N 7RB. (SAE appreciated.)

Instituto de Proprietarios Extranjeros, Avda de Ifach 1, Edificio el Portál, Calpe (Alicante). Institute of Foreign Property Owners.

Spanish National Radio, 16 Berners St, London W1. Tel: (0207) 631 1238.

Spanish and Portuguese Jews Congregation, Lauderdale Road Synagogue, 2 Ashworth Road, London W9. Tel: (0207) 289 2573.

Spanish and Portuguese Synagogue, Holland Park, 8 St James Gardens, London W11. Tel: (0207) 603 3232.

Spanish Catholic Chaplaincy, 47 Palace Court, London W2. Tel: (0207) 229 885.

Spanish Commercial and Technical Translations, Marzell House, 116 North End Road, London W14. Tel: (0207) 486 3476.

Spanish Speaking Services, 138 Eversholt St, London NW1. Tel: (0207) 388 1732.

Spanish Technical Translations Co, 76 Shoe Lane, London EC4. Tels: (0207) 583 8690, 353 5813. (Translators, interpreters, printers.)

Spanish Technical Translation Service, 219 Mortlake Road, Richmond. Tel: (0208) 876 7721.

Spanish Technical Translators, 11 Uxbridge Road, London W12. Tel: (0208) 749 3211.

Spanish Television, 16 Berners St, London W1. Tel: (0207) 631 3706.

Spanish Translations, 64 Queens St, London EC4. Tel: (0207) 248 8707.

CONSUMER AFFAIRS

Edward McMillan-Scott MEP, Parliamentary Office, Ref EDG004, European Parliament, Rue Belliard, Brussels 1040. Tel: (965) 20 50 00.

FAB – Foreign Advice Bureau, calle Cruz 5, Torremolinos (Málaga). Tels: 952 383022, 383653, 388736.

Ombudsman (*Defensor del Pueblo*), Señor don Alvaro Gil Robles, calle Eduardo Dato 31, 280210 Madrid. Tel: 91 319 40 38, 308 28 06.

OMIC (Oficina Municipal de Información al Consumador). Complaints and Information. Local.

Organización de Consumidores y Usarios (OCU), Edocusa, calle

Jerez 3-portal C-2° B, 28016 Madrid. Tel: 91 457 52 07. Fax: 91 457 06 60.

Union de Consumidores de Espana (UCE), Apd 53238, 28080 Madrid. Tel: 91 435 42 52, 435 46 13. (Head office.)

FOREIGN LANGUAGE PUBLICATIONS PRODUCED IN SPAIN

See pages 24–25 for listings.

PERIODICAL PUBLISHERS

Costa Golf, Apartado 358, Loma de los Riscos 1, Torremolinos (Málaga). Tel: 952 38 15 42. (Monthly.)

Green Digest Espana, Glorieta de Pérez Cidón 1-1°B, 28027 Madrid. Tel: 91 742 74 44, 742 79 53. Fax: 91 320 40 16.

Sur in English, Avda Doctor Marañon 48, 29009 Malaga. Tel: 952 64 96 67, 952 64 96 92. Fax: 952 61 12 56.

Glossary of
Useful Words and Phrases

MONEY

¿Cuánto es?	How much is that?
¿Cuánto vale?	How much is this? (in a shop).
¿Cuánto debe?	How much do I owe you? (in a bar).
¿La dolorosa, por favor?	A very Spanish way of getting the bill and a little old-fashioned which may suggest you have been in the country longer than in actuality.
La cuenta, por favor.	The bill, please (in a restaurant).
¿Para qué es esta cantidad?	What's this amount for?
¿Está incluido el IVA?	Does that include VAT?
¿Acepta usted esta tarjeta de crédito?	Do you accept this credit card?
Quédese con el cambio.	Keep the change.
Traígame la hoja de reclamación.	Bring me a complaint form.

TRAVEL

Se me ha averiado el coche.	My car's broken down
¿Qué distancia hay hasta . . . ?	How far is it to . . . ?
¿Dónde hay una gasolinera?	Where is there a petrol station?
Llénemelo, por favor.	Fill the tank please.
Siga todo derecho.	Keep straight on.
¿Hay un aparcamiento cerca de aqui?	Is there a car park near here?
¿Puede arreglar este pinchazo?	Can you fix this puncture?
¿Dónde está la playa?	Where's the beach?
correos?	the post office?
la estación?	the station?
el hotel?	the bank?
el teatro?	the theatre?
¿Dónde puedo cambiar dinero?	Where can I change money?

¿Es éste el tren para Madrid?	Is this the train for Madrid?
¿Hace falta cadenas de nieve?	Are snow chains necessary?
Mil pesetas de gasolina, por favor.	1,000 pts worth of petrol please.
¿Tiene agua/aire/aceite?	Have you water/air/oil?
Quiero alquilar un coche para una día	I want to hire a car for a day.
una semana	a week
Tengo carnet de conducir.	I have a driving licence.
Pídame un taxi, por favor.	Please call me a taxi. (Give the taxi driver the written address and show him a map.)
¿Hay un autobús al (desde el) aeropuerto?	Is there a bus to (from) the airport?

HOTELS AND ACCOMMODATION

Hemos reservado una habitación doble.	We have booked a double room.
¿Tiene una habitación individual?	Do you have a single room?
¿doble?	double room?
Quiero una habitación con baño.	I want a room with a bath.
con ducha.	with a shower.
con vista.	with a view.
¿Tiene aire acondicionado?	Is there air-conditioning?
¿Puedo ver la habitación?	May I see the room?
¿A que hora se cena?	When is dinner served?
¿Tiene servicio de habitación?	Do you have room service?
dormitonio	bedroom
cama individual	single bed
calefacción	central heating
No molestar	Do not disturb
Cortesia de la dirección	With the compliments of the management
En caso de incendio, salir por la salida de socorro más cercana	In event of fire, please use the nearest emergency exit

GENERAL

giro postal	postal order
hacienda	tax office
declaración	tax return form
entrega personal	personal delivery (by hand)
correo certificado	registered post

Aduana	Customs and Excise
permanencia	permit allowing a stay of a further three months in Spain
residencia	residence permit
certificado de antecedentes penales	certificate of good conduct
matricula	number plate
autovía	bypass
autopista	motorway
salida	(motorway) exit
estación de servicio	service station
límite de velocidad	speed limit
letra	form of hire purchase
talón	cheque
caja de ahorros	savings bank
Insalud	Spanish national health service
gasolinera	petrol filling station
comisaría	police station
gestor	official dealing with paperwork
Telefonica	the name of the Spanish telephone service
alcalde	mayor
ayuntamiento	town hall
papel de estado	tax stamp(s)
permisos	permits
permiso de conducción	driving licence
abogado	lawyer
notario	notary
derechos	duties to pay
impuesto	tax
seguro	insurance
contrato	contract
el alquiler	the rent
Quiero alquilar un piso.	I want to rent a flat
¿Conoce uno?	Do you know of one?
Se alquila	for rent
Se vende	for sale
hipoteca	mortgage
escritura (de compraventa)	house conveyance document
Registro de Propriedad	Property Register
Bachillerato	secondary education
Bachiller	school matriculation certificate
formación	training

ABBREVIATIONS

RENFE (Red Nacional de Ferrocarriles Españoles)	State Railway
Cia (Compania)	company
c/ (calle)	street
EE UU (Los Estados Unidos)	USA
ETA (Euzkadi Ta Askatsuna)	Basque Independence Organisation
GC (Guardia Civil)	Civil Guard
Vd/s (Usted/es)	you (the polite form for an official or a person you do not know well)
IVA	VAT (Value Added Tax)
ITV (Inspección Técnico de Vehiculos)	the Spanish MOT test
SA (Societa Anonima)	a Spanish company

Further Reading

There is a host of books available on all aspects of Spanish regional history, culture and geography, as well as travel guides and books on food and drink. Selections can be found at many local bookshops and libraries, as well as at internet bookshops such as www.amazon.co.uk, www.bol.com, www.bookshop.co.uk, www.thebookplace.com.

For Spanish language sites, try www.es.bol.com and the Spanish site at www.amazon.com.

A very brief selection of further reading is included below:

TRAVEL GUIDES & COMPANIONS

There are numerous national and regional guides, updated at intervals, including: AA, Berlitz, City Guides, Companion Guides, Everyman, DK Travel Guides, Fodor's, Insight Guides, Let's Go, Lonely Planet, Michelin Guides, Rough Guides, Time Out. There are also a number of companions to Spain, including:

Jones, Harold Dennis. *Where to Go in Spain* (Settle, 1988). 156pp illustrated paperback with maps.

Marvin, Garry. *Coping with Spain* (Basil Blackwell, 1990). 181pp, hardback and paperback with illustrations.

Morris, Jan. *Spain* (Penguin Books, 1986). A companion to Spain – its history, its physiognomy, its temperament and intellect and its culture.

Robertson, Ian. *Spain: Blue Guide* (Black, 2001). 598pp, illustrated paperback, with maps.

ARTS OF SPAIN

Benarde. *Spanish Ceramic Designs* (Stemmer House (US), 1984). 48pp, paperback, with 82 illustrations.

Franco, J (ed). *Spanish Short Stories: Parallel Text* (Penguin, 1970). Paperback.

Homage to Barcelona: the City and Its Art. 1888-1936 (Arts Council, 1985). 328pp, illustrated paperback.

Jordan, Barry. *Writers and Politics in Franco's Spain (Influence of Politics 1936-1960)* (Routledge 1990). 240pp. Hardback.

Kraus, Dorothy. *The Gothic Choirstalls of Spain* (Routledge and Kegan Paul, 1986). 192pp, illustrated hardback.

Mackay, David. *Modern Architecture in Barcelona. 1854-1939* (BSP Professional, 1989). 119pp, illustrated paperback, with maps.

Newmark (Ed). *Dictionary of Spanish Literature* (Greenwood Press, 1972). 352pp, hardback.

Northup. *Introduction to Spanish Literature* (University of Chicago Press, 1960). 532pp, paperback.

Oliveira, Cezar Claudia. *Madrid Arts Guide* (Art Guide, 1989). 109pp, illustrated paperback, with maps.

Palomino. *Lives of the Eminent Spanish Painters and Sculptors* translated from the Spanish by N A Mallory (Cambridge University Press, 1988). 423pp, illustrated hardback.

Romanillos, Jose L. *Antonio de Torres: Guitar Maker: his Life and Work* (A Nadder Book, 1987). 240pp, illustrated hardback.

Schwartz. *Spanish Film Directors 1950-85: Twenty One Profiles* (Scarecrow Press, 1986). 253pp, paperback with 133 illustrations.

Takacs, *Spanish Genre Painting in the Seventeenth Century* translated from Hungarian Akad Kiado (Budapest, 1983). 283pp, illustrated hardback.

Ward, Philip. *Oxford Companion to Spanish Literature* (Oxford University Press, 1978). 638pp, hardback.

PALACES

Brown, Jonathan. *A Palace for a King: The Buen Retiro and the Court of Philip IV (Madrid)* (Yale, 1986). 320pp, illustrated paperback.

Rosenthal, Earl E. *The Palace of Charles V in Granada* (Princeton University Press, 1985). 320pp, illustrated hardback, with 61 plates.

Trevelyan, Raleigh. *Shades of the Alhambra (Granada)* (The

Folio Society, 1984). 127pp, illustrated. (Secker and Warburg, 1985), 128pp, illustrated.

GEOGRAPHY OF SPAIN

Busselle, Michael. *Landscape in Spain* (Pavilion, 1988). 159pp, illustrated, photographs by Michael Busselle, commentary by Nicholas Luard.

Casa Valdes, Marquesa de. *Spanish Gardens* translated from the Spanish by Edward Tanner (Antique Collectors' Club, 1987). 299pp, illustrated, with maps.

Rose, David. *Beneath the Mountains: Exploring the Deep Caves of Asturias* (Hodder & Stoughton, 1987). 192pp, illustrated, with maps, 8 colour plates.

LIVING IN SPAIN

Ballard, Sam and Jane. *Paradores of Spain: Unique Lodgings in State-owned Castles, Convents, Mansions and Hotels* (Moorland, 1986). 241pp, illustrated paperback, with maps.

Blackstone Franks Guide to Living in Spain (Kogan Page, 1988). 208pp, with map.

Brown, Karen. *Spanish Country Inns and Paradors* (Harrap Columbus, 1987). 272pp, illustrated paperback.

Busselle, Michael. *Castles in Spain: A Traveller's Guide featuring the National Parador Inns* (Pavilion, 1989). 239pp, illustrated with maps.

Kite, Cynthia. *Spanish Country Inns and Paradors* (Columbus, 1987). 256pp, illustrated paperback, with maps.

Reay-Smith, John. *Living in Spain* (Hale, 1986). 207pp, illustrated, with maps, and 16 plates.

Spanish Property: A Buyer's Bible (McMillan, Bennett, 1988). 40pp, paperback, with map.

Svensson, Per. *Your Home in Spain: Before and After Purchase* (Institute of Foreign Property Owners, 1987). 200pp, illustrated paperback, with one map. 3rd edition.

Tinsley, Teresa. *Time Off in Spain and Portugal* (Horizon, 1989).

Williams, N Scarlyn. *Teach Yourself Spanish* (Edinburgh University Press, 1966).

NATURAL HISTORY

Busby, John. *Birds in Mallorca* (Christopher Helm, 1988). 128pp.

Grunfeld, Frederic V. *Wild Spain: A Travellers and Naturalists Handbook* (Ebury, 1988). 222pp, illustrated paperback, with maps.

Innes, Clive. *Wild Flowers of Spain* (Cockatrice, 1987). 64pp, illustrated paperback.

Polunin, Oleg. *Flowers of South-West Europe: A Field Guide* (Oxford University Press, 1988). 480pp, illustrated paperback, with maps.

Tomkies, Mike. *In Spain's Secret Wilderness* (Cape, 1989). 224pp, 32 plates, and colour photographs.

SPANISH FOOD AND DRINK

Aris. *Recipes from a Spanish Village* (Conran Octopus, 1990). 144pp, illustrated.

Azner and Froud. *Home Book of Spanish Cooking* (Faber, 1974). 224pp, paperback.

Begg, Desmond. *Traveller's Wine Guide to Spain* (Aurum Press, 1998) 144 pp.

Butcher. *Spanish Kitchen* (Macmillan, 1990). 320pp, illustrated.

Evans, Sarah Jane. *Travellers Guide to the Spanish Menu* (Absolute Press, 1985). Paperback.

Fahy. *Little Spanish Cook Book* (Appletree Press, 1990). 60pp, with 30 colour illustrations.

Gustafson, S. *Cheap Eats in Spain* (Chronicle Books, 2000).

Jessell. *Taste of Spain: Traditional Spanish Recipes and their Origins* (IB Tauris, 1990). 160pp, colour illustrations.

Radford, John. *The New Spain: A companion to contemporary Spanish wine.* (Mitchell Beazley, 1998) 224pp.

Read, Jan. *Pocket Guide: Wines of Spain* (Mitchell Beazley, 2001). 298pp, illustrated.

Snell. *202 Spanish Wines* (Lookout Publications, Spain 1987). 124pp, illustrated paperback.

Sterling, Richard and Jones, Allison. *Lonely Planet World Food: Spain* (Lonely Planet Publications, 2000) 302 pp.

Scarborough, Ron. *Rioja and its Wines* (Survival Books Ltd, 2000) 213 pp.

Stewart, Carole. *Self-catering in Spain: Making the Most of the*

Local Food and Drink (Croom Helm, 1986). 144pp, illustrated paperback.

PERSONAL ACCOUNTS OF LIFE IN SPAIN

A Day in the Life of Spain. Photographed by 100 of the world's leading photo journalists on one day, May 7th 1987 (Collins, 1988). 220pp, chiefly illustrations, with maps.

Borrow, George. *The Bible in Spain: Or, the Journeys, Adventures, and Imprisonments of an Englishman in an Attempt to Circulate the Scriptures in the Peninsula* (originally published John Murray, 1843) (Century Travellers Series, 1985). 510pp, paperback. This is a fascinating account of journeys in Spain some 150 years ago. The writing is beautifully descriptive and religion is kept to a minimum. Many of the comments on politicians, regional characteristics, personalities in the public eye, and general conditions are as true today as then and help to explain the lack of education and knowledge that still exists. It is written from the point of view of a much travelled Englishman. One admires his courage.

Braithwaite, Belinda. *A Girl, a Horse and a Dog* (Collins, 1988). 236pp, illustrated, with 12 plates and 1 map.

Brenan, Gerald. *South from Granada* (originally published Hamish Hamilton, 1957) (Folio Society, 1988). 278pp, 14 leaves of plates.

Chetwode, Penelope. *Two Middle-Aged Ladies in Andalusia* (originally published John Murray, 1963) (Century Travellers Series, 1985). 288pp, illustrated paperback.

Davies, Hugh Seymour. *The Bottlebrush Tree: A Village in Andalusia* (Constable, 1988). 208pp.

Gala, Antonio. *El Manuscrito Carmesi* (Planeta, Spain 1990). A Spanish best-seller treating of the Conquest of Granada from the point of view of the last Arab ruler.

Hooper, John. *The Spaniards: a Portrait of the New Spain* (Viking, 1986). 288pp, illustrated, with maps.

Lee, Laurie. *As I Walked Out One Midsummer Morning 1935-36* (Deutsch, 1969). 191pp, illustrated, with map.

Lewis, Norman. *Voices of the Old Sea (1945-50) (Catalonia)* (Hamish Hamilton, 1984). 202pp.

Luard, Nicholas. *Andalucia: A Portrait of Southern Spain (1972-1980)* (Century, 1985). 288pp, illustrated paperback.

Luke, Peter. *The Mad Pomegranate & The Praying Mantis: an Andalusian Adventure (1967-1977)* (Mantis, 1984). 238pp.

Macaulay, Rose. *Fabled Shore: From the Pyrenees to Portugal* (originally published Hamish Hamilton, 1949) (Oxford University Press, 1986). 248pp, illustrated paperback, with 8 plates.

Morris, Ian. *Spain* (originally published Faber, 1979) (Barrie and Jenkins, 1988). 207pp, colour illustrations and 1 map.

O'Brien, Kate. *Farewell Spain (1936-37)* (originally published Heinemann, 1937) (Virago, 1985). 229pp, illustrated with drawings.

Pritchett, V.S. *The Spanish Temper* (Hogarth Press, 1984). 224pp, paperback.

Walker, Ted. *In Spain* (Secker & Warburg, 1987). 280pp, 1 map.

Winsland, Elaine. *Ibiza Was My Home* (Book Guild, 1989). 180pp, illustrated.

SOCIAL AND POLITICAL HISTORY

Blinkhorn, Martin. *Spain in Conflict 1931-1939: Democracy and Its Enemies* (Sage, 1986). 304pp, illustrated.

Borkenau, Franz. *The Spanish Cockpit: An Eyewitness Account of the Political and Social Conflicts of the Spanish Civil War* (Liberation Classics) (originally published Faber, 1937) (Pluto, 1986). 320pp, paperback.

Carr, Raymond. *The Civil War in Spain (1936-39)* (Weidenfeld & Nicolson, 1986). 328pp, paperback, with maps.

Clark, Bob. *No Boots to my Feet: Experiences of a Britisher in Spain 1937-38* (Student Bookshops Ltd, 1984). 120pp, illustrated paperback.

Collins, Roger. *The Arab Conquest of Spain: 710-797 (A History of Spain)* (Basil Blackwell, 1989). 239pp.

Cunningham, Valentine (ed). *Spanish Front: Writers on the Civil War* (Oxford University Press, 1986). 320pp, illustrated paperback.

Dillard, Heath. *Daughters of the Reconquest: Women in Castilian Town Society 1100-1300* (Cambridge University Press, 1984). 272pp, illustrated.

Edmonds Lloyd. *Letters from Spain* ed Amirah Inglis (Allen and Unwin, 1985). 216pp, illustrated with 1 map.

Fletcher, R A. *The Quest for El Cid* (Hutchinson, 1989). 220pp, illustrated, with maps.

Foweraker, Joe. *Making Democracy in Spain: Grass Roots Struggle in the South 1955-1975* (Cambridge University Press, 1989). 289pp, with 1 map.

Fusi-Aizpurua, Juan Pablo. *Franco: A Biography* translated by Felipe Fernandez-Armesto (Unwin Hyman, 1987). 202pp, illustrated, with maps.

Gilmour, David. *The Transformation of Spain: From Franco's Dictatorship to the Constitutional Monarchy* (*1939-1984*) (*Quartet, 1985*). 320pp.

Gregory, Walter. *The Shallow Grave: A Memoir of the Spanish Civil War* (Gollancz, 1986). 192pp, illustrated, with maps.

Gunther, Richard. *Spain after Franco: The Making of a Competitive Party System* (University of California Press, 1988). 509pp, illustrated paperback, with map.

Haigh, R H, Morris, D S, and Peters, A R (eds). *The Guardian Book of the Spanish Civil War* (Wildwood House, 1987). 332pp, with maps.

Irving, Washington. *Chronicles of the Conquest of Granada* (Oxford University Press, 1829).

Krasikov, Anatalii. *From Dictatorship to Democracy: Spanish Reportage* translated by N Shartse (Pergamon, 1984). 227pp, illustrated.

Lalaguna, Juan. *A Travellers History of Spain* line drawings by John Hoste (Windrush, 1990). Illustrated paperback.

Lancaster, Thomas D, and Prevost, Gary (eds). *Politics and Change in Spain* (Praeger, 1985). 224pp, illustrated, with 1 map.

Lovett, A W. *Early Habsburg Spain 1517-1598* (Oxford University Press, 1986). 300pp, paperback, with maps.

Martin, Colin, and Parker, Geoffrey. *The Spanish Armada* (Penguin, 1989). 269pp, illustrated paperback.

Martin Paula. *Spanish Armada Prisoners: The Story of the Nuestra Senora del Rosario and her Crew, and of other prisoners in England 1587-97* (Exeter University Publications, 1988). 113pp, illustrated.

Matthews, John. *El Cid: Champion of Spain* plates by James Field (Firebird, 1988). 48pp, illustrated with 1 map.

Mattingley Garrett, *The Defeat of the Spanish Armada* (Cape, 1983). 384pp, illustrated. 2nd edition.

McDonogh, Gary Wray. *Good Families of Barcelona: A Social History of Power in the Industrial Era* (Princeton University Press, 1986). 262pp, illustrated, with maps.

McKee, Alexander. *From Merciless Invaders: The Defeat of the Spanish Armada* (Souvenir, 1987). 288pp, illustrated, with maps.

Milne-Tyte, Robert. *Armada! The Planning, the Battle and After* (Hale, 1988). 160pp, paperback, with maps.

Noel, Gerard. *Ena, Spain's English Queen* (Constable, 1984). 323pp, illustrated.

Orwell, George. *Homage to Catalonia: And, Looking Back on the Spanish War* (Penguin in Association with Secker and Warburg, 1966, 1984 printing). 246pp, paperback.

Parker, Geoffrey. *Philip II* (originally published Hutchinson, 1979) (Cardinal, 1988). 238pp, paperback with 1 map.

Pollack, Benny. *The Paradox of Spanish Foreign Policy: Spain's International Relations from Franco to Democracy* (Pinter, 1987). 200pp.

Preston, Paul (ed). *Revolution and War in Spain 1931-1939* (Methuen, 1986). 299pp, paperback.

Preston, Paul. *The Triumph of Democracy in Spain* (Methuen, 1986). 288pp, paperback.

Pridman, Geoffrey. *The New Mediterranean Democracies: Regime Transition in Spain, Greece and Portugal (1975-1983)* (Cass, 1984). 193pp, illustrated, with maps.

Rubottom, R Richard. *Spain and the United States: Since World War II* (Praeger, 1984). 163pp.

Share, Donald. *The Making of Spanish Democracy* (Praeger, 1986). 230pp.

Smyth, Denis. *Diplomacy and Strategy of Survival: British Policy and Franco's Spain 1940-41)* (Cambridge University Press, 1988). 560pp.

Stradling, R A. *Philip IV and the Government of Spain 1621-1665* (Cambridge University Press, 1988). 615pp, illustrated, with 1 map.

SPANISH ECONOMICS AND LAW

Credades, Bernado M (ed). *Spanish Business Law* (Kluwer Law & Taxation, 1985). 656 pp.

Donaghy, P J, and Newton, Michael T. *Spain: A Guide to Political and Economic Institutions* (Cambridge University Press, 1987). 242pp, illustrated paperback.

Harris, Robert Joseph. *The Spanish Economy in the 20th Century* (Croom Helm series on the contemporary economic history of Europe, 1985). 207pp.

Ringrose, David R. *Madrid and the Spanish Economy 1560-1850* (University of California Press, 1983). 405pp, illustrated, with maps.

Sanchez-Albornoz, Nicolas. *The Economic Modernization of Spain 1830-1930* translated by Karen Powers and Manuel Sanudo (New York University Press, 1987). 295pp, illustrated, with 1 map.

Tamames, Ramon. *The Spanish Economy: An Introduction* (Hurst, 1986). 274pp, illustrated, with maps.

RELIGION

Christian, William A. *Local Religion in Sixteenth Century Spain* (Princeton University Press, 1989). 283pp, illustrated paperback, with map.

Lannon, Frances. *Privilege, Persecution and Prophecy: The Catholic Church in Spain 1875-1975* (Clarendon, 1987). 350pp, with 2 maps.

Payne, Stanley G. *Spanish Catholicism: An Historical Overview* (University of Wisconsin Press, 1984). 263pp.

BULLFIGHTING

Collins, Larry and Lapierre, Dominique. *Or I'll Dress you In Mourning (El Cordobes)* (Weidenfeld and Nicolson, 1968, 1988 printing). 349pp, illustrated paperback, with 24 plates.

Marvin, Garry. *Bullfight* (Basil Blackwell, 1988). 244pp, illustrated.

Index

GETTING A JOB IN EUROPE
The guide to finding short or long-term employment in Europe
Mark Hempshell

Whether you're seeking executive, professional, skilled or casual work, this information-packed guide is a must. Discover how to job search, how to apply (and prepare Euro CVs), and find out what working life in Europe is really like. It is full of key contacts, sample documents and hard-to-find information.

192 pages. 1 85703 353 6. 4th edition

GETTING A JOB ABROAD
The handbook for the international jobseeker: where the jobs are, how to get them
Roger Jones

Now in its fifth edition, this is the handbook for anyone planning to spend a period of work abroad. Includes a wide range of reference addresses covering employment agencies, specialist newspapers, a comprehensive booklist and helpful addresses. '. . . lots of hard information and a first class reference section.' *Escape Committee Newsletter.*

336pp. illus. 1 85703 418 X. 5th edition

SPENDING A YEAR ABROAD
A guide to opportunities for self-development and discovery around the world

Nick Vandome

'Unlike most reference books this one should be read right through, and that is a pleasure as well as being very informative . . . totally comprehensive.' *School Librarian Journal.*

176 pages. 1 85703 544 5. 4th edition

LIVING & WORKING IN GREECE
Your guide to a successful short or long-term stay

Peter Reynolds

Now in its second edition, Peter Reynolds' comprehensive guide gives you an overview of this beautiful country and guides you through procedures, paperwork, travel and accommodation options. Discover what jobs are available, how self-employment works, and how to set up your own business. Take a glimpse at everyday life too – everything from health, welfare and sport, to recreation, leisure and education. 'This informative handbook guides the newcomer through all the procedures they need to know.' *Athens News.*

144 pages. 1 85703 657 1. 2nd edition